From Christianity to a True Believer

From Christianity to a True Believer

SAME-SEX RELATIONS AND THE BIBLE

Anita L Nottuh

Enlighten Publishing House, LLC
32406 Franklin Rd., Suite 250018
Franklin, MI 48025

From Christianity to a True Believer
Second Edition, Revised 2017

All scriptures were taken from the *King James Version* (KJV) of the Bible.
Words have been changed, deleted or added for clarity.

The Truth

The truth does not care who it offends,
what it offends, or why it offends.
—*Anita L Nottuh*

CONTENTS

Introduction

What is Christianity?

Many see Christianity today as a religion that is born out of the Bible. However, if you ask anyone what religion he or she belongs to, no one would say Christianity. The reason is: Christianity is a banner that encompasses many different religious sects (churches), such as Baptist, Catholic, Jehovah's Witness, Lutheran, Presbyterian, Non-denominational, and many others. Although they are all different, they all have a common ideology, that Jesus Christ is their standard-bearer. Each religious sect has its own unique followers, true believers who share the same views and beliefs concerning worship, personal beliefs, values, and much more. They are called Christians. A Christian, by definition, is a follower of Jesus Christ. However, according to the *Holman Bible Dictionary*, there is a deeper meaning for those who call themselves Christians.

> **"CHRISTIAN:** The Greek *Christianos* originally applied to the slaves belonging to a great household. It came to denote the adherents of an individual or party. A Christian is an adherent of Christ; one committed to Christ; a follower of Christ."

Many Christians come to know God and Christ through the New Testament Bible. Those within the Christian community believe the written words of the Bible were God-inspired or actually are God's words given through men. Paul, the predominant character and writer of the New Testament, give Christians' one view of God in fourteen books. They are Romans, 1 Corinthians, 2 Corinthians, Galatians, Ephesians, Philippians, Colossians, 1 Thessalonians, 2 Thessalonians, 1 Timothy, 2 Timothy, Titus, Philemon, and

Hebrews. In all, the New Testament Bible appears to have been written by eight men: Matthew, Mark, Luke, John, Paul, Peter, James, and Jude. It is the writings of these men about God and Christ that more than likely determine Christians' overall perception of who God is.

SAME-SEX RELATIONS

When the topic is same-sex relations, many in the Christian community cite scriptures from the Bible demonizing it. This can be a learned response because many Christians are taught from the pulpit to believe that same-sex relations are wrong. However, what is not taught or explained by the church is the covenant of love between two men, Jonathan and David.

Many Christians believe that God and Jesus are against same-sex relations because of how it is mentioned negatively in the Bible. The greatest amount of confusion against same-sex relations comes from two books. The first is Leviticus in the Old Testament, which was said to be written by Moses. The second is Romans in the New Testament, which was said to be written by Paul (formerly known as Saul), also known as the Apostle Paul.

Many in the Christian community justify their attitude and views against same-sex relationships using these two verses in the Old Testament law.

Leviticus 18:22

You shall not lie with mankind, as with womankind: it is (an) abomination.

Leviticus 20:13

If a man also lie with mankind, as he lieth with a woman, both of them have committed an abomination: they shall surely be put to death; their blood shall be upon them.

Having a law and understanding the law are two different things. There must be a need for the law and the law must do what it is designed to do. To understand the laws in Leviticus as they are written in the scriptures, it is necessary to ask the following questions: To whom were the laws given? What is the purpose for the laws? Who would the laws protect and how? If the laws in Leviticus were exclusively about same-sex relations, why were woman not included? These are some of the questions that need to be answered in order to understand what the laws were all about.

The main scriptures used against men and women in a same-sex relationship in the New Testament come from two verses in Romans, which are weighted more heavily because the Old Testament is considered to be obsolete for Christians today.

Romans 1:26

> For this cause God gave them up to vile affections: for even their women did change the natural use into that which is against nature:

Romans 1:27

> Likewise the men, leaving the natural use of the woman, burned in their *lust* one toward another; men with men working that which is unseemly, and receiving in themselves that recompense of their error which was meet.

There is a stark difference between Romans 1:26–27, and the Old Testament laws in Leviticus 18:22 and Leviticus 20:13. The laws written in Leviticus apply only to men, whereas, Paul's letter to the

Romans included both women and men. Why? Did God change? Did God inspire Paul (thousands of years later) to include women? These are some of the questions that must be considered in order to get to the truth about Paul and why he wrote what he did in Romans 1:26-27. Many will be surprised to learn from Paul's own writings that he had a problem with *lust*, which he dealt with deceptively by blaming his own actions on sin, the law, and God.

WHY WORDS MATTER

You may have heard this saying, "Sticks and stones can brick my bones, but words can never hurt me." It is one of the greatest lies ever told because words are the reason for someone to want to hit or beat you with a stick or a stone, other than being mentally unstable.

Many pastors, preachers, teachers, reverends, bishops, doctors, and priests (church leaders), Christians, non-Christians, researchers, students, and many others use biblical reference materials for additional information or a better understanding of a topic. Many people believe or would like to believe that reference materials such as dictionaries and encyclopedias provide factual information about a subject, title, or word. This is not always the case when it comes to biblical reference materials such as the *Wycliffe Bible Encyclopedia*, the *Holman Bible Dictionary*, and many others on the topics related to same-sex relations. In some instances, they are actually trying to persuade you the reader or researcher to believe or accept a certain point of view, not always the truth. This is why reference materials are reviewed and examined in this book in order to present a clear picture of what the Bible actually says compared to what others want you to believe the Bible says.

Out of the entire Bible, four verses matter most on the subject of same-sex relations. They are as follows:

Old Testament Verses

Leviticus 18:22
> You shall not lie with mankind, as with womankind: it is (an) <u>abomination</u>.

Leviticus 20:13

If a man also lie with mankind, as he lieth with a woman, both of them have committed an <u>abomination</u>: they shall surely be put to death; their blood shall be upon them.

New Testament Verses

Romans 1:26

For this cause God gave them up to vile affections: for even their women did change <u>the natural use</u> into that which is against nature:

Romans 1:27

And likewise also the men, leaving <u>the natural use</u> of the woman, burned in their lust one toward another; men with men working that which is unseemly, and receiving in themselves that recompense of their error which was meet.

These four verses matter because they can actually destroy lives, especially Romans 1:26–27. Not just the lives of men and women in or desiring a same-sex relationship or marriage, but the lives of those who believe that same-sex relations are wrong and worthy of death based on three words, "the natural use." These three words imply that the actions of men and women who have same-sex relations are somehow unnatural, therefore according to Paul, worthy of death!

If all the laws today were changed to stop discrimination against men and women in a same-sex relationship or marriage, they would only be free under the law. Many church leaders are not preaching and teaching the truth as it relates to the Bible, especially on the topic of same-sex relations. Therefore, spiritual men and women in or desiring a same-sex relationship or marriage may believe that they are condemned as well as Christians spiritually believing that men and women who have same-sex relations are worthy of death!

The very reasons for this book, subtitled: *Same-Sex Relations And The Bible*, is to let people know that they are not condemned. It is to challenge those with predisposed ideologies against men and women in or desiring a same-sex relationship or marriage with actual scriptures. Also, to answer most questions that may arise on the topic of same-sex relations and beyond, which in turn will lead you on a journey to discover other aspects of the Bible.

PART 1

CHAPTER 1

JONATHAN AND DAVID

———

THE ONLY TRUE STORY in the entire Bible that could shed light on a same-sex relationship is the love story of David (before and after he became king) and King Saul's son, Jonathan. In order to establish whether God gave up on men and women who are in a same-sex relationship, as Paul described in Romans 1:26–27, is to determine how God felt about David. Jonathan and David's love story is powerful. It has all the trapping of a great love story today. It has intrigue, jealousy, deceit, plots of murder, and suspense *intertwined* between two books, First and Second Samuel in the Old Testament. Their love story begins with Jonathan's actions toward David and ends with David's own words and actions for and about his love, Jonathan. If you find that God gave up on David, then what Paul wrote could be true. If not, what Paul wrote would be a lie.

THE COVENANT OF LOVE

1 Samuel 17:58–18:4

> Saul said to him: Whose son are you, young man? David answered: I am the son of Jesse. Then it came to pass, **that the soul of Jonathan was knit with the soul of David, and Jonathan loved him as his own soul. Then Jonathan and David made a covenant, because he loved him as his own soul. Then Jonathan stripped himself of the robe that was upon him, and gave it to David, and his garments, even to his sword, and to his bow, and to his girdle.**

JEALOUSY

1 Samuel 18:5-9

> David went where Saul sent him, and behaved himself wisely: and Saul set him over the men of war, and he was accepted in the eyes of all the people and also Saul's servants. Then it came to pass that the women came out of all cities of Israel, singing and dancing, to meet King Saul, with tabrets, with joy, and with instruments of music. And the women answered one another as they played, and said, Saul has slain his thousands, and David his ten thousands. And Saul was very angry, because the saying displeased him; and he said, they have ascribed to David ten thousands, and to me they have ascribed but thousands and what can he have more but the kingdom? And Saul eyed David from that day and forward....

JONATHAN STOOD WITH DAVID

1 Samuel 19:1–10

Saul spoke to Jonathan his son, and to all his servants, that they should kill David. However, Jonathan Saul's son delighted much in David. So, Jonathan told David, that his father sought to kill him. Then Jonathan spoke well of David to his father, and said to him, let not the king sin against his servant, David; because he has not sinned against you. Saul listened to Jonathan and swore, as the LORD live, David shall not be killed. Then Jonathan brought David to Saul, and he was in his presence, as in times past. And the evil spirit from the LORD was upon Saul, as he sat in his house with his javelin in his hand...and Saul sought to smite David to the wall with the javelin; but he slipped away out of Saul's presence, and he smote the javelin into the wall: and David fled, and escaped that night....

1 Samuel 20:1–13

David fled and went to Jonathan and said: What have I done? What is my iniquity? What is my sin before your father, that he seek my life? Jonathan said to him, God forbid; you shall not die: My father will do nothing either great or small without letting me know. Why would, my father hide his intentions from me? Then David swore and said, **your father certainly know that I have found grace in your eyes; and he says, let not Jonathan know, least he be grieved, but truly as the LORD live and as your soul shall live, there is but a step between me and death. Then Jonathan said to David, whatsoever your soul desire, I will do it for you.** Then David said to

Jonathan, tomorrow is the new moon, if your father misses me, then say: David earnestly asked leave of me that he might return to Bethlehem his city. If he say, it is well; I shall have peace: but if he is very angry, then be sure that evil is determined by him against me. **Therefore you should deal kindly with me; for you have brought me into a covenant of the LORD with you.** Jonathan replied, if I knew for certain that evil were determined by my father against you, would I not tell you? Then send you away that you may go in peace and the Lord be with you as he has been with my father.

JONATHAN'S LOVE FOR DAVID CHALLENGED

1 Samuel 20:25–34

The king sat upon his seat, as at other times by the wall, and David's seat was empty. Saul noticed David's seat was empty, but said nothing. The next day which was the second day of the month, again David's seat was empty and Saul said to Jonathan his son: Why has David not come to eat with us, neither yesterday, nor today? Jonathan said to Saul: David earnestly asked leave of me to go to Bethlehem to be with his family… therefore, he is not at the king's table. **Then Saul's anger was kindled against Jonathan, and he said to him, you son of the perverse rebellious woman, do not I know that you have chosen the son of Jesse to your own confusion, and to the confusion of your mother's nakedness?** For as long as the son of Jesse (David) live upon the ground: you shall not be established, nor your kingdom. Now fetch him, for he shall surely die. Jonathan answered Saul his father, and said to him: Why should he die? What has he done? Then Saul cast a javelin at his son, Jonathan to kill him. Now, because of Saul's actions, Jonathan knew his father was determined to kill David. So, Jonathan arose from the table in fierce anger and did not eat for he was grieved for David, because his father had done him shame.

THE SECRET TRYST

1 Samuel 20:35–42

In the morning, Jonathan went out into the field to meet David at the appointed time (which was planned out before hand with the young lad), accompanied by a young lad. He said to the boy, run and find the arrows which I will shoot. As the boy ran, Jonathan shot an arrow beyond him. When the boy had reached the place of the arrow which Jonathan had shot, Jonathan yelled out to the boy (which was code words to David), and said: Is an arrow beyond you? Then Jonathan called out to the boy, saying hurry up, stay not. The boy then gathered up all the arrows, and came to Jonathan. (However, the boy did not know that Jonathan was there to meet David). Then Jonathan gave his artillery to the boy, and said to him, go, carry them back to the city. As soon as the boy was gone, **David appeared and fell on his face to the ground and bowed himself three times and they kissed one another, and wept one with another, but David wept even more. Then Jonathan said to David go in peace, we have sworn both of us in the name** of the LORD, saying, the LORD be between me and you, and between my seed and your seed for ever. David rose up and departed and Jonathan returned to the city.

The Second Covenant

1 Samuel 23:15–18

David saw that Saul had come to seek his life, while he was in the wilderness. **Then Jonathan went to David and strengthened his hand in God and said to him, fear not: the hand of my father shall not find you and you shall be king over Israel, and I shall be next to you and that, Saul, my father already knows. Then they made a covenant before the LORD** and David abode in the woods and Jonathan went to his house…

The death of King Saul and his son Jonathan

1 Sam 31:2, 6

… The enemy of Israel followed hard upon Saul and his sons and they were all killed: Jonathan and two other sons belonging to Saul…. Therefore, Saul and his three sons all died in the same day….

2 Sam 1:11-12

David took hold on his clothes, and tore them and likewise all the men that were with him. They mourned, and wept, and fasted until the evening, for Saul, and for Jonathan his son, and for the people of the LORD, and for the house of Israel; because they were fallen by the sword.

2 Samuel 1:17

David lamented with this lamentation over Saul and over Jonathan his son...

2 Samuel 1:22–27

From the blood of the slain, from the fat of the mighty, the bow of Jonathan turned not back, and the sword of Saul returned not empty. Saul and Jonathan were lovely and pleasant in their lives, and in their death they were not divided: they were swifter than eagles, they were stronger than lions. Daughters of Israel, weep over Saul, who clothed you in scarlet, with other delights, who put on ornaments of gold upon your apparel. How are the mighty fallen in the midst of the battle! O Jonathan, you were killed... I am distressed for you: **My brother Jonathan, very pleasant have you been to me: <u>your love to me was wonderful, passing the love of women.</u>**

Note: The story of Jonathan and David: The full story: *1 Samuel 17:57 - 2 Samuel 21:14,* intertwined between both books.

ABOUT JONATHAN

When you closely examine the love story of Jonathan and David from Jonathan's perspective, you will see that the relationship between them was of a sexual nature. Their love story began with Jonathan's soul being knit with the soul of David because Jonathan was in love with David. The very next thing that happened was Jonathan and David made a covenant. Why a covenant? Perhaps the word "covenant" was used to show that David was in agreement with the love Jonathan gave him. However, it still does not explain why they would make a covenant. The details were never mentioned, but the reason for the covenant was love. What follows their covenant is what makes it sexual in nature. When Jonathan stripped naked before David, removing his robe, which was an outer covering over his garments. Then Jonathan removed his garments, including his sword, bow, and girdle. Now ask yourself: What man strips naked before another man after professing his love for him and it not be sexual?

Many will rely upon the fact that the story of Jonathan does not say explicitly that he had sex with David. However, the Bible does not say explicitly that Adam and Eve had sex, yet they had a son named Cain. In fact, the scripture used the word "knew" to imply a sexual interaction between Adam and Eve.

Genesis 4:1
> Adam knew Eve his wife; and she conceived, and bare Cain, and said, I have gotten a man from the LORD.

Therefore in the same vein that you would accept the word "knew," which implied sex between Adam and Eve, could be the same frame of mind to accept David's own words toward Jonathan saying, "your love to me was wonderful, passing the love of women," which could imply a sexual relationship.

Now again, why a covenant? Could this covenant between Jonathan and David be their attempt at a same-sex marriage? A covenant, by definition, is an agreement. So are marriages, where the husband and wife to be, both agree to love, honor and cherish each other, in sickness and in health. When you take a closer look at the relationship between Jonathan and David, their covenant could resemble that of a same-sex relationship or marriage. In 1 Samuel 18:1, the word "knit" was used to describe the souls of Jonathan and David to imply that their souls were intertwined or had become one. It's another way of saying they were soul mates. This resembles what Jesus said concerning marriage itself.

Matthew 19:5–6

> **For this cause shall a man leave father and mother, and shall cleave to his wife: and they two shall be one flesh? Wherefore they are no longer two, but one flesh.**

The man and his wife are not physically joined together. What is being said is figurative, meaning their hearts and souls are in agreement and they become as one, in other words "knitted." What follows in 1 Samuel 18:3 was the covenant between Jonathan and David because he loved him. Then in 1 Samuel 18:4, Jonathan stripped naked before David. Could this be the beginning stages of them con-summating their same-sex marriage? If no, what other reason could there be for Jonathan to make a covenant of love with David and then remove all his clothing?

1 Samuel 18:1

> The soul of Jonathan was knit with the soul of David, and Jonathan loved him as his own soul…

1 Samuel 18:3–4

> Then Jonathan and David made a covenant, because he loved him as his own soul. Then Jonathan stripped himself of the robe that was upon him, and gave it to David, and his garments, even to his sword, and to his bow, and to his girdle.

What give credence to a relationship on David's part between him and Jonathan, was his own words. Why compare the love of another man to the love of all women except to make a distinction?

2 Samuel 1:26

> …your love to me was wonderful, passing the love of women.

What could further support the relationship between Jonathan and David as a same-sex relationship or marriage is based on who Jonathan was. When King Saul was angry and challenged his son Jonathan and his relationship with David, calling him "confused" and then comparing his confusion with a woman's naked body, this statement alone implied that King Saul under-stood his son Jonathan's relationship with David to be of a sexual nature.

1 Samuel 20:30

> You son of the perverse rebellious woman, do not I know that
> you have chosen the son of Jesse to your own confusion, and
> to the confusion of your mother's nakedness?

Nevertheless, Jonathan was a man who stood in his own truth. He was willing to separate himself from David forever, if that was what it took to save his life. Jonathan cemented his love for David when they made the second covenant, that David shall be king over Israel, while his own father was yet the king of Israel. Jonathan was not confused: he had chosen the son of Jesse. He remained steadfast and stood with David, protected him, gave him comfort, and would have laid down his own life, for his love. The love story of Jonathan and David is exactly what Jesus taught to his disciples in the gospel of John.

John 15:12–13

> **This is my commandment, that you love one another,
> as I have loved you. Greater love has no man than
> this: that a man lay down his life for his friends.**

Jesus did not quantify how or whom you should love, but, that you love. Notice, Jesus did not say that a man lay down his life for his wife, mother, father, sister, brother, or children, but "friends." Jonathan and David were friends who loved one another. One could only imagine what Paul would have thought of David saying about another man "your love to me was wonderful, passing the love of women" or that David made a covenant of love with Jonathan, another man. It is not clear what Paul knew about David because he did not include anything specific about his life in any of his writings. Therefore, it is more than likely that Paul knew very little about David. However, did Paul know God?

God, the creator of heaven and earth is seen among both Christians and non-Christians as omnipresent, meaning God is everywhere; the Alpha and the Omega, meaning God is the beginning and the end; and all-knowing, meaning God knows all things, including the heart of David.

Now, if what Paul wrote in Romans 1:26–27 about God was true, then why would God appoint David king over Israel and say that David was a man after his own heart?

Acts 13:21–23

> They desired a king: God gave them Saul the son of Cis, a man of the tribe of Benjamin, for forty years. When he had removed him, he raised up David to be their king; to whom he gave testimony, and said, I have found David the son of Jesse, a man after my own heart, which shall fulfil all my will. Of this man's seed has God according to his promise raised to Israel a Savior, Jesus.

According to the Old Testament scriptures, God loved, protected, and supported David throughout his entire life, before and after he became king and beyond. After King David's death, God appointed David's son, Solomon, to reign as king after him.

Therefore, God who is believed to be all-knowing and omnipresent did not give up on David after he entered into a covenant of love with another man because he loved him. On the other hand, what about Jesus? Paul began his letter to the Romans saying that Jesus was made after the seed of David.

Romans 1:3
> Concerning his Son Jesus Christ our Lord, which was made of the seed of David according to the flesh…

If David was wrong for being in love with another man, would Jesus, the Son of God, have stood by him? In the book of Revelations, it is written that Jesus wanted everyone to know that he was of the seed of David. According to the scriptures, Jesus gave a declaration from heaven concerning David. Saying,

Revelations 22:16
> **I Jesus have sent my angel to testify to you these things in the churches. I am the root and the off-spring of David, and the bright and morning star.**

Therefore, if God did not have a problem with David and Jesus did not have a problem with David, then why should anyone else have a problem with David or any other man whose love for another man is greater than his love for women? Many will accept that there is something more than a friendship or brotherly love between Jonathan and

David based on their love story as a whole and the words spoken by David from his heart.

2 Samuel 1:26

My brother Jonathan: very pleasant have you been to me: <u>your love to me was wonderful, passing the love of women.</u>"

CHAPTER 2

THE COVENANT

———

THE REASON FOR THIS CHAPTER is to show how the *Holman Bible Dictionary* and the *Wycliffe Bible Encyclopedia* saw Jonathan and David's relationship and how far they would go to try to explain it.

When you search the *Holman Bible Dictionary* and the *Wycliffe Bible Encyclopedia* for additional information or an explanation about the covenant between Jonathan and David, what you will find is vague and ambiguous information or nothing at all.

THE WYCLIFFE BIBLE ENCYCLOPEDIA

When you search the word "covenant" in the *Wycliffe Bible Encyclopedia*, there are approximately six pages on the subject; however, the covenant between Jonathan and David was not mentioned. When you search the name "Jonathan" for information related to the covenant between him and David, this is a portion of what you will find.

JONATHAN

* *"His friendship with David.* Jonathan and David's friendship is a most inspiring epic. After David slew the Philistine giant Goliath and

won for himself a permanent place in the royal court, Jonathan loved the shepherd lad with all his soul. He recognized that David was a man chosen for the throne of Israel. He acquiesced to this by making a covenant and presenting to David his own princely robe and armor (1 Sam 18:1-4)."

❧ "The final and romantic conference between these friends took place in the wilderness. There they made a pact that when David became the next king, Jonathan would be his prime minister, and they renewed their covenant to protect each other's posterity forever."

If you only read the first paragraph, you would walk away with the understanding that Jonathan and David were just friends. However, once you look further to the next paragraph, the author/writer used the word "romantic" in describing what took place between friends. The word "romantic" is defined in different ways, however, it usually means one thing when one confesses his love toward the other and it leads to a covenant of love.

"**Romantic:** 1. involving sexual love: involving or characteristic of a love affair or sexual love, especially when the relationship idealized or exciting and intense. 2. suitable for love: characterized by or suitable for lovemaking or the expression of tender emotions"
Encarta ® World English Dictionary

The *Wycliffe Bible Encyclopedia* appears to be saying that the covenant between friends was based on David becoming king and Jonathan, his prime minister. First of all, nowhere in the King James Version (KJV) or the New International Version (NIV) Bibles does the title "prime minister," appear.

Secondly, what Jonathan actually said to David was this, "and you shall be king over Israel, and I shall be next to you," which meant forfeiting his place to the throne for David. Jonathan being the son of a king would have been next in line to the throne. Therefore, Jonathan putting David first implied they would be together, hence the phase "I shall be next to you." Now ask yourself: What man would make a covenant to relinquish the power and prestige of being a king, for just a friend?

When you search the name "David" in the *Wycliffe Bible Encyclopedia* for information related to the covenant between him and Jonathan, this is what you will find:

DAVID

* "There friendship was of one soul in two bodies. The bond which united Jonathan and David was - mainly their common faith in the covenant of love of God for Israel. This unity of spirit won Jonathan to David, and he made with him a covenant of friendship and exchanged gifts in token of that friendship (1Sam 18:1-4)."

In searching the name David, you are given a different answer from when the name Jonathan was searched. The *Wycliffe Bible Encyclopedia* appears to be saying Jonathan and David made a covenant of friendship because of "their common faith in the covenant of love of God for Israel," which was why they exchanged gifts. The only problem with this scenario is there was no exchange of gifts. According to the scriptures, Jonathan's soul was knitted with the soul of David. They made a covenant because Jonathan loved David, and then Jonathan stripped naked before David, giving him all his clothing. Ask yourself: What did David give to Jonathan?

1 Samuel 18:1–4

> The soul of Jonathan was knit with the soul of David, and Jonathan loved him as his own soul. Then Jonathan and David made a covenant, because he loved him as his own soul. And Jonathan stripped himself of the robe that was upon him, and gave it to David, and his garments, even to his sword, and to his bow, and to his girdle.

Why make up different answers, is it because the *Wycliffe Bible Encyclopedia* refuses to acknowledge that Jonathan, a man, was in love with David, also a man?

THE HOLMAN BIBLE DICTIONARY
"Covenant: a pact, treaty, alliance, or agreement between two parties of equal or of unequal authority."

When you search the word "covenant" in the *Holman Bible Dictionary* for information related to Jonathan and David's relationship, this is what you will find:

COVENANT

* "Jonathan and David cut a covenant of friendship in which Jonathan acknowledged David's right to the throne (1 Sam. 18:3; 23:18). Such an agreement was a "covenant of the Lord" (1 Sam

20:8), that is the Lord was its witness and guarantee. At the time Jonathan possessed greater authority than David, but in the covenant he acknowledged David's coming authority over him."

The *Holman Bible Dictionary* cited three different scriptures (1 Sam. 18:3, 20:8, 23:18) to support its assertion that the covenant between Jonathan and David was one of friendship and a "covenant of the Lord," based on Jonathan relinquishing the power and prestige to be king, to David.

First, who "cuts" an agreement to be friends?

Second, Jonathan and David made two covenants, which were both before the Lord. When you look closely at 1 Samuel 20:8, it is vague all by itself. Although it supports and confirm the fact that Jonathan and David's covenant of love, was a covenant of the Lord, according to David's own words, which one could conclude that Jonathan and David more than likely had a same-sex relationship or marriage.

The First Covenant

I Samuel 18:3
  Then Jonathan and David made a covenant, because he loved him as his own soul.

Then David said to Jonathan (reminding him of their covenant of love),

1 Samuel 20:8
  Therefore you shall deal kindly with me; for you have brought me into a covenant of the LORD with you.

The *Holman Bible Dictionary* seems to be a little misleading using 1 Samuel 20:8 in relations to Jonathan relinquishing his right to the throne for David. Jonathan and David made a second covenant in 1 Samuel 23:17-18, concerning David being king.

The Second Covenant

1 Samuel 23:17-18
> You shall be king over Israel, and I shall be next to you; and that also Saul my father knows and they two made a covenant before the LORD...

To be absolutely clear, 1 Samuel 20:8 is referring to the first covenant between Jonathan and David, not the second covenant.

Finally, let's just accept that because Jonathan was next in line to be king he had some authority over David. Again, what man would agree to relinquish his authority, power and the prestige of being king for just a friend?

The *Wycliffe Bible Encyclopedia* and the *Holman Bible Dictionary* both give a more protected and yet subtle account concerning Jonathan and David's relationship, saying they were friends. Well, lovers can be friends and many are.

CHAPTER 3

THE LAW

IN ORDER TO UNDERSTAND THE Old Testament law, as it relates to Leviticus 18:22 and Leviticus 20:13, it is necessary to know to whom the laws were given and why.

According to the scriptures, the laws and the commandments were given to the descendants of Jacob. Jacob was a person whose name appeared to have been changed from Jacob to Israel. You may recall God saying, "I am the God of Abraham, Isaac and Jacob." It is this Jacob, who had twelve sons with four different women: Leah, her sister Rachel, Zilpah (Leah's handmaid), and Bilhah (Rachel's handmaid).

Genesis 35:23–26

> The sons of Leah; Reuben, Jacob's firstborn, and Simeon, and Levi, and Judah, and Issachar, and Zebulun: The sons of Rachel; Joseph, and Benjamin: The sons of Bilhah, Rachel's handmaid; Dan, and Naphtali: The sons of Zilpah, Leah's handmaid; Gad, and Asher: these are the sons of Jacob...

It would appear, that the descendants of Jacob became the children of Israel, God's chosen people, who were also known as the twelve tribes of Israel and the Israelites.

The Lord God gave the laws to Moses to give to the children of Israel to live by. This included Leviticus 18:22 and Leviticus 20:13, which were composed of statutes, ordinances, and judgments. These laws, which are among many, were given to the children of Israel after they were removed from slavery in Egypt, but before they entered the Promised Land (Canaan) so they would know how to conduct themselves in the land God gave them as an inheritance.

Leviticus 18:1–4

> The LORD spoke to Moses, saying, Speak to the children of Israel, and say to them, I am the LORD your God....the land of Egypt, where you were...and the land of Canaan, where I bring you...neither shall you walk in their ordinances. You shall do my judgments, and keep my ordinances, to walk in: I am the LORD your God.

WHY THE LAWS?

It is commonly preached that Leviticus 18:22 and Leviticus 20:13 is about consensual same-sex relations.

Leviticus 18:22
> Thou shall not lie with mankind, as with womankind: it is (an) abomination.

Leviticus 20:13
> If a man also lie with mankind, as he lieth with a woman, both of them have committed an abomination: they shall surely be put to death; their blood shall be upon them.

For a better understanding of both laws, you must make some assumptions because both laws were written by men and for men, and they are poorly written and somewhat vague. When you look at both laws as they are written, in Leviticus 18:22, you must believe or accept that the word "you," which means "you," refers to men. Also in Leviticus 18:22 and Leviticus 20:13, you must believe or accept that the word "lie" or "lieth," means "to have sex" or "have a sexual interaction." This understanding is necessary to comprehend the scriptures as they are written.

Now to truly believe that Leviticus 18:22 and Leviticus 20:13 were solely about consensual same-sex relations, then women having sex with other women should have been a part of the law. Then again, maybe it was more acceptable for women to have sex with other women. Abraham had more than one wife, and his first wife Sarah was his father's daughter. Abraham's son Jacob had many wives and concubines, King David had multiple wives, and his son Solomon had seven hundred wives and three hundred concubines.

To be clear, the Old Testament does not mention women being with or wanting other women sexually or anything close to it within the King James Version of the Bible. This is why it is important to take a closer look at each law thoroughly, first Leviticus 18:22 and then Leviticus 20:13, to understand why women were not included.

LEVITICUS 18:22

You shall not lie with mankind, as with womankind:

it is (an) <u>*abomination*</u>.

To be absolutely clear, Leviticus 18:22, is saying that a man should not have sex with another man because it is an abomination. The use of the word "abomination" says to the reader that two men having sex is shameful, something horrible, disgusting, and immoral. Now Leviticus 18:23, the very next statute or ordinance says the following:

Leviticus 18:23

Neither shall you (men) lie with any beast to defile yourself with: neither shall any woman stand before a beast to lie down with: it is confusion.

To be absolutely clear, Leviticus 18:23, is saying that a man or a woman should not have sex with a beast or an animal (bestiality), because it is confusion. When comparing Leviticus 18:22 with Leviticus 18:23, you can see that the law pertaining to lying with a beast or an animal included both men and woman. Now this tells us women could have been included in Leviticus 18:22, if it was necessary. Therefore Leviticus 18:22 is <u>not</u> about consensual same-sex relations, but something else.

When you take a closer look at Leviticus 18:23, by definition, confusion is a state of being confused. Being confused is a state of mind or a situation that lacks clarity. When you analyze Leviticus 18:23 as it is written, confusion is the reason given that a man or a woman should not have sex with a beast or an animal. Now the question is:

Confusion for whom? A man having sex with a beast or an animal knows exactly what he is doing! Likewise, a woman having sex with a beast or an animal knows exactly what she is doing! Once again: Confusion for whom?

Now you would have to believe that the Lord God said to Moses, "Say to the children of Israel, a man should not have sex with another man because it is shameful, something horrible, disgusting, and immoral. Neither should a man or woman have sex with a beast or an animal because it lacks clarity." Now again, if there was no confusion concerning a man or woman having sex with a beast or an animal, would bestiality be accepted as the norm?

Genesis 2:18–24

> The LORD God said, it is not good that the man should be alone; I will make a help mate for him. Then out of the ground the LORD God formed every beast of the field and every fowl of the air and brought them to Adam to see what he would call them, and what Adam called every living creature, that was their name. Adam gave names to all cattle, and to the fowls of the air and to every beast of the field, but for Adam there was not found a help mate for him. Then the LORD God caused a deep sleep to fall upon Adam, and while he slept, he took one of his ribs… and the rib, which the LORD God had taken from Adam, he made a woman, and brought her to him. Adam said, this is now bone of my bones, and flesh of my flesh: she shall be called Woman, because she was taken out of Man. Therefore shall a man leave his father and his mother, and shall cleave to his wife: and they shall be one flesh.

Was it the Lord God's intention for Adam to find a help mate or a partner among the animals? It was Adam who did not find the beast of the field or any creatures of the earth acceptable. Therefore, only as an afterthought did the Lord God make the woman, not from the dust of the earth, as he did with Adam and all the beast and creatures of the field and air, but separate, from a man's rib. Then the Lord God brought the woman to Adam as he did all the beast of the field and the creatures of the earth, and she was acceptable to him. So, why all the disdain as it relates to two men having sex compared to bestiality?

LEVITICUS **20:13**

If a man also lie with mankind, as he lieth with a woman,
both of them have committed an <u>abomination</u>: they shall
surely be put to death; their blood shall be upon them.

To be absolutely clear, Leviticus 20:13, is saying that a man should not have sex with another man, and in doing so, they have done something shameful, horrible, disgusting, and immoral and should be put to death for their actions. Now looking forward to Leviticus 20:15–16 (a rewrite of Leviticus 18:23) which state the following:

Leviticus 20:15-16

> If a man lie with a beast, he shall surely be put to death: and you shall kill the beast. If a woman approach any beast, and lie down, you shall kill the woman, and the beast: they shall surely be put to death; their blood shall be upon them.

To be absolutely clear, Leviticus 20:15–16, is saying a man or a woman should not have sex with a beast or an animal (bestiality), and in doing so, the man or woman, along with the beast or animal, should be put to death. When comparing Leviticus 20:13 with Leviticus 20:15–16, you can see that the law pertaining to lying with a beast or animal also included both men and woman. Again this tells us women could have been included in Leviticus 20:13 (a rewrite of Leviticus 18:22), if it was necessary. Therefore Leviticus 20:13 is <u>not</u> about consensual same-sex relations, but something else.

When you compare Leviticus 18:22 with Leviticus 20:13, you would have to believe or accept that the Lord God had a change of mind and said to Moses, "Say to the children of Israel, if a man has sex with another man, it is still an abomination (meaning it is shameful, something horrible, disgusting, and immoral), and both of them should be put to death."

Now, when you compare Leviticus 18:23 with Leviticus 20:15–16, you would have to believe or accept that the Lord God changed his mind again and said to Moses, "Now say to the children of Israel, if a man or a woman have sex with a beast or an animal, it is no longer confusion (based on Lev 20:15-16), but it is still <u>not</u> an abomination, and they should both be put to death." Now the question is: Why does the Lord God consider a man having sex with another man an abomination, compared to a man or a woman having sex with a beast or an animal?

Just as in modern times, laws are made to prevent or allow certain behaviors. In order to understand the laws of Leviticus 18:22 and Leviticus 20:13, it is necessary to know what the Bible says happened on the earth, which affected only the men and warranted death. Just maybe we are to take Leviticus 18:22 or Leviticus 20:13 literally. In the New Testament, Paul gives us another way of looking at the law.

Romans 3:20
>   Therefore by the deeds of the law there shall no flesh be justified in his sight: for by the law is the knowledge of sin.

If this is true, the law is the knowledge of sin, meaning the law was created to bring sin to the light. Then the law itself exposes sin. So, what sin did Leviticus 18:22 or Leviticus 20:13 expose?

CHAPTER 4

SODOM AND GOMORRAH

———◆———

The story of Sodom and Gomorrah is one of the most epic and destructive acts in the Bible, which destroyed both human life and land. The one thing that comes to mind at the mentioning of Sodom and Gomorrah is God's judgment, raining down fire and brimstone upon the wicked out of heaven like bombs. God even destroyed the land for which men stood and left it desolate to this day, as a reminder that God's anger was kindled against such a vile and vicious people.

Genesis 19:24–25
> Then the LORD rained upon Sodom and upon Gomorrah brimstone and fire from the LORD out of heaven; He overthrew those cities, and all the plain, and all the inhabitants of the cities, and that which grew upon the ground.

Many people have heard of the destruction of Sodom and Gomorrah and how epic it was. The cause for the destruction is vague and taught in different ways. Much of what is preached from the pulpit and taught throughout the Christian community is that God's wrath or vengeance was against consensual same-sex relations. This is simply not true. However, some will always blame God's wrath upon

Sodom and Gomorrah on consensual same-sex relations and nothing else. When you read the story of Sodom and Gomorrah, one thing is clear. It's not about men having or wanting consensual same-sex relations with other men. It is about rape.

THE STORY OF SODOM AND GOMORRAH

Genesis 18:20–19:29

There came two angels to Sodom. Lot seeing them rose up to meet them; and he bowed himself with his face toward the ground and said come into my house, and stay all night, and wash your feet, and in the morning go your way, and they said No, we will stay in the street all night. Then he pressed upon them greatly and they entered into his house. Then the men of the city, even the men of Sodom, surrounded the house, both old and young. They called Lot, and said to him: Where are the men that came into your house this night? Bring them out to us, that we may know them. Lot went out the door to them, and shut the door after him, and said, do not this wicked thing. Now, I have two virgin daughters, let me bring them out to you, and do to them what is good in your eyes: only to these men do nothing, because they came under the shadow of my roof. They said to Lot, stand back....now will we deal worse with you, than with them and came near to break down the door, but the men/angels put forth their hand, and pulled Lot into the house with them, and shut the door. Then the men/angels struck the men that were at the door of the house with blindness, both small and great that they could not find the door. Then the men/angels said to Lot, are there any others here besides you: son-in-law, sons, or daughters? Bring them out: for we will destroy this place, because the cry of them is waxen great before the face of the LORD and the LORD has sent us to destroy it. Take your wife, and two daughters, which are here and leave; least you be consumed in the iniquity of the city.... Then the LORD rained upon Sodom and upon Gomorrah brimstone and fire out of heaven and overthrew those cities, and all the plain, and all the inhabitants of the cities, and that which grew upon the ground.

The Laws

It should be absolutely clear that the story of Sodom and Gomorrah is not about men choosing to have consensual same-sex relations. It's about rape. Since God intervened, technically what happened in Sodom and Gomorrah can only be described as attempted sexual rape. For clarity, when the statement is made in Genesis 19:5, "bring them out to us, that we may know them," it implies raping them. In this instance the word "know" in the biblical sense means "to have sex." In Genesis 19:5, the word "know" is used in the present tense, whereas in Genesis 4:1, it was used in the past tense.

Genesis 4:1

And Adam <u>knew</u> Eve his wife; and she conceived, and bare Cain...

During the time of Sodom and Gomorrah, there were no statutes or ordinances, according to the scriptures. Therefore, it made sense for God who destroyed two cities, Sodom and Gomorrah, with fire and brimstone from heaven to include a commandment (You Shall Not Covet) and laws going forward that would tell his people what they should or should not do.

Leviticus 18:22

You shall not lie with mankind, as with womankind: it is abomination.

Leviticus 20:13

If a man also lie with mankind, as he lieth with a woman, both of them have committed an abomination: they shall surely be put to death; their blood shall be upon them.

To be clear, Leviticus 18:22 and Leviticus 20:13, was never about consensual same-sex relations, but rape. What was happening in Sodom and Gomorrah with men raping or wanting to rape other men was why Leviticus 18:22 and Leviticus 20:13 was needed. Remember, in the story of Sodom and Gomorrah, Lot protected the men, who were strangers, but offered both his virgin daughters in their place to be gang-raped by all the men of the city. This alone made it clear from Lot's point of view, that it was an abomination to rape a man, but acceptable to rape a woman, which would clarify why women were not included in both laws.

Therefore, according to the law a man being raped would be seen as an abomination: something horrible, shameful, disgusting and immoral. In addition, the pervasive acts of rape alone would explain the change of mind as to why death was warranted, in Leviticus 20:13.

A Closer Look Leviticus 20:13

When you take a closer look at Leviticus 20:13 as it is written, there is something not quite right about the words "both of them." It may be that the law is just poorly written, but it deserves a second look as it relates to Sodom and Gomorrah because the rapists and the victims would all be put to death.

Leviticus 20:13

> If a man lie with mankind, as he lieth with a woman, **both of them** have committed an abomination: they shall surely be put to death; their blood shall be upon them.

When you look at all the statutes, ordinances, and judgments given to the children of Israel, it appears as though Leviticus 20:13 would be in conflict with other laws, making it difficult to carry out God's punishment, which is death. For instance, several laws state that, to be put to death, there must be two or three witnesses to the crime at hand.

Numbers 35:30

> Whosoever kills any person, the murderer shall be put to death by the mouth of witnesses: but one witness shall not testify against any person to cause him to die.

Deuteronomy 17:6–7

> At the mouth of two witnesses, or three witnesses, shall he that is worthy of death be put to death; but at the mouth of

one witness he shall not be put to death. The hands of the witnesses shall be first upon the accused to put him to death, and afterward the hands of all the people, so that the evil is put away from among you.

Deuteronomy 19:15
One witness shall not rise up against a man for any iniquity, or for any sin, at the mouth of two witnesses, or at the mouth of three witnesses, shall the matter be established.

Analyzing Leviticus 20:13 from the standpoint of Sodom and Gomorrah encompassing all the statutes, ordinances, and judgments, the law makes no sense. To be clear, when a man is raped, he would need at least one or two witnesses to stand with him for the rapist(s) to be punished (put to death).

Now strictly looking at Leviticus 20:13, if there were two or more witnesses willing to accuse the rapist(s) of the act, both the man who is raped and his rapist(s) would all be put to death. In this case, the righteous victim would be put to death with the unrighteous rapist(s). Then no man who is raped would turn to the authority for anything but pray that there were no witnesses!

Now apply the words "both of them" with two men in a consensual same-sex relationship. When you consider all the statutes, ordinances, and judgments, under what circumstances could anyone be found out or prosecuted under Leviticus 20:13 as it is written, short of a public display, which would be suicide?

For example:

1. If two men home alone engaged in a private sexual act or activities, there are no two or three witnesses to the act itself, only God, who is said to be all-knowing and omnipresent. If God chose not to act, by putting "both of them" to death, then God's own statute or ordinance is null and void.

2. If two men home alone engaged in a private consensual sexual act or activities and another man sees them and accuses them, the law is not satisfied by only one witness. Even if two or more witnesses see them but don't accuse them of breaking the law, nothing happens, and there is no punishment. The statute or ordinance given to them is null and void. Remember, the witnesses must, in essence, throw the first stone in putting the accused to death, and there is no penalty for not reporting them.

All statutes, ordinances, and judgments must make sense, especially when they are said to have come from God, or inspired by God. If you remove Leviticus 20:13 from the Old Testament, nothing changes. Therefore, the law is useless, and no one can be helped or protected by it.

Why would God give a law to anyone that was useless? Only God would know when two men were engaged in a private consensual sexual act. So, why would God who is said to be omnipresent and all-knowing, need two or three witnesses (men) to accuse men of having consensual sex?

Why would God rely on men to carry out judgments? When it is said that God gave the statutes, ordinances, and laws, you expect that God is able to perform what God says. Remember Sodom and Gomorrah when the people cried out. God rained down fire and brimstone upon the ungodly from heaven, according to the scriptures. God is still on the throne. Therefore, God, who gave the statutes and ordinances to the children of Israel through Moses, should have been the same God who was judge and executioner, putting "both of them" or "all of them" to death for the statutes and ordinances God deemed were broken. Then Leviticus 20:13 would literally make sense.

THE COMMANDMENT
(YOU SHALL NOT COVET)

The Ten Commandments were given directly by God to the children of Israel, so, they would know how to conduct themselves before God and with each other in the Promised Land.

Deuteronomy 4:13-14
> He declared to you his covenant, which he commanded you to perform, ten commandments; and he wrote them upon two tables of stone. The LORD commanded me (Moses) at that time to teach you statutes and judgments, that you might do them in the land you are going to possess.

Looking closely at the commandments written in Exodus, chapter 20, they are a prohibitive set of commands telling the children of Israel what they should not *do*, with two exceptions: Obey the Sabbath and Honor your mother and father. The first four commandments, established the prohibited behavior of the children of Israel, as they relate to God. The remaining prohibited commandments established the conduct among the children of Israel as to how they relate to one another.

- You shall have no other gods before me (Exo. 20:3)
- You shall not make any graven image (Exo. 20:4)
- You shall not bow down, nor serve them (Exo. 20:5)
- You shall not take the Lord's name in vain (Exo. 20:7)
- Obey the Sabbath (Exo. 20:8)
- Honor your mother and father (Exo. 20:12)
- You shall not kill (Exo. 20:13)

- ❧ You shall not commit adultery (Exo. 20:14)
- ❧ You shall not steal (Exo. 20:15).
- ❧ You shall not bear false witness (Exo. 20:16)
- ❧ You shall not covet (Exo. 20:17)

You Shall Not Covet

What does the commandment, You Shall Not Covet, mean? It is the cause of much confusion because it is vague in its meaning and poorly written. Nowhere in the Old Testament does it define what "coveting" actually is. Some think of desire and nothing else. To desire is to want or wish very strongly for someone or something. The word "covet" is defined in different ways and can mean a variety of things. For example:

> **"Covet:** Is to desire wrongfully, inordinately,
> or without due regards to the rights of others."
> *Webster's Encyclopedic Unabridged Dictionary*

———◆———

> **"Covet:** To want somebody else's property:
> to have a strong desire to possess something
> that belongs to somebody else"
> *Encarta ® World English Dictionary*

Taking both definitions into account, the commandment, You Shall Not Covet, as it relates to property, is the desire to possess wrongfully property, without due regards to the rights of others. However, in the New Testament, Paul's letter to the Romans made the commandment, You Shall Not Covet, about lust.

Romans 7:7
     …for I had not known lust, except the law had said, You shall not covet.

The word "lust" is also defined in different ways and can mean a variety of things. For example:

> "**Lust:** is an intense sexual desire or appetite or
> uncontrolled illicit sexual desire or appetite."
> *Webster's Encyclopedic Unabridged Dictionary*

———

> "**Lust:** sexual desire: the strong physical desire
> to have sex with somebody, usually without
> associated feelings of love or affection"
> *Encarta ® World English Dictionary*

Taking both definitions into account, the commandment, You Shall Not Covet, as it relates to lust, is an uncontrolled illicit sexual desire or appetite to have sex with someone, usually without associated feelings of love or affection. Now the question is: Do the scriptures support both descriptions of the commandment, You Shall Not Covet, as it relates to property and lust? Yes. Looking closely at the commandment, You Shall Not Covet, it appears to be two separate commandments in one, meaning two different things.

Exodus 20:17

> You shall not covet thy neighbor's house, you shall not covet thy neighbor's wife, nor his manservant, nor his maidservant, nor his ox, nor his ass, nor any thing that is thy neighbor's.

(First Half)
> You shall not covet thy neighbor's house.

(Second Half)
> You shall not covet thy neighbor's wife, nor his manservant, nor his maidservant, nor his ox, nor his ass...

The first half of the commandment begins, You Shall Not Covet thy Neighbors house. This part of the commandment makes the entire commandment about property. This is where confusion comes in and many think of desire (to want or wish very strongly for someone or something), for the entire commandment. You Shall Not Desire, makes no sense. Desiring your neighbor's house or anything that belongs to your neighbor is not a bad thing. To desire what belongs to your neighbor to the point of taking ownership unlawfully is. However, that would fall under the commandment, You Shall Not Steal. If the commandment, You Shall Not Covet meant only strong or wrongful desire, there would be no need for any other commandment. For example: No man commits adultery without having a strong desire to do so. The same would be true for all the other commandments. Therefore, to covet cannot simply be to desire wrongfully someone else's house or property. Nor can it be simply stealing, because You Shall Not Steal is a commandment already. You must physically do something in order to break the commandments. So the question is: How does one covet someone else's house or property? The scriptures give us two examples to help answer this question, the first in the book of Joshua and the second in the book of Micah.

#1

In the book of Joshua, a man by the name of Achan confessed his sin of violating the commandment of God, by coveting. What Achan did that was considered coveting in his confession was to wrongfully desire and possess property that belonged to someone else. What should stand out about Achan's confession is the phrase "among the spoils." The use of the word spoils implies the property was taken by force or violence.

Joshua 7:20-21

> Achan answered Joshua, and said, Indeed I have sinned against the LORD God of Israel, and thus and thus have I done: When I saw among the spoils a goodly Babylonish garment, and two hundred shekels of silver, and a wedge of gold of fifty shekels weight, then **I coveted them,** *and* **took them**; and, behold, they are hid in the earth in the midst of my tent, and the silver under it.

#2

The book of Micah, is another example, where a man's property is taken by force or violence.

Micah 2:1-2

> Woe to them that devise iniquity, and work evil upon their beds! When the morning is light, they practice it, because it is in the power of their hand. **They covet fields,** *and* **take them by violence**; and houses, and take them away: so they oppress a man and his house, even a man and his heritage.

Therefore, taking everything into account, You Shall Not Covet, as it relates to property is to "take by force" wrongly what belongs to someone else. This is deviant behavior, which can be described as rape.

"Rape: 4. an act of plunder, violent seizure, or abuse; despoliation;
violation 5. the act of seizing and carrying off by force"
Webster's Encyclopedic Unabridged Dictionary

Now, the commandment, You Shall Not Covet, is known as the tenth
commandment. Paul's focus was not on the first half of the commandment, which relates to property, but the second half, which
relates to human beings and living things.

The second half of the commandment states, You Shall Not Covet
your neighbor's wife, nor his manservant, nor his maidservant, nor
his ox, nor his ass (donkey). This makes sense, as to how lust can be
applied. Looking at the second half of the commandment, You Shall
Not Covet, from Lot's point of view makes things much clearer.

Lot had men with uncontrolled illicit sexual desires at his door,
threatening him with violence and wanting to take hold of the two
witnesses (men) who entered into his house, so they could rape them.

Therefore, taking everything into account, You Shall Not Covet as it
relates to lust is to "take by force" sexually what belongs to someone
else. This is deviant sexual behavior, which also can be described as
rape. In the case of Sodom and Gomorrah attempted (physical) rape.

"Rape: 1. The crime of having sexual intercourse
with a person forcibly and without consent"
Webster's New World Compact

—◆—

"**Rape:** 1. is the unlawful compelling of a person through physical force or duress to have a sexual interaction."
Webster's Encyclopedic Unabridged Dictionary

Now, if you change the word "Covet" to "Rape" for the entire tenth commandment, then, You Shall Not Rape thy neighbor's house and You Shall Not Rape thy neighbor's wife, nor his manservant, nor his maidservant, nor his ox, nor his ass, makes sense.

CHAPTER 5

YOU SHALL NOT RAPE

———

In the book of Judges, there is a story about a Levite man and his concubine. This story should seem very familiar to you because it mirrors the story of Sodom and Gomorrah in many aspects, but with a totally different outcome.

In the story of Sodom and Gomorrah, God heard their cries and acted by raining down fire and brimstone on the ungodly. After which, God remembered their cries and gave the commandment, You Shall Not Covet and the laws, Leviticus 18:22 and Leviticus 20:13 to prohibit that behavior. However, to what effect? The story, The Concubine is heartbreaking and yet eye-opening. The only thing that comes to mind after reading this story is: Where was God?

An Important Note: This story has been shortened and words have been added, deleted or changed to make the story readable. When you read the story of the Levite and the concubine in the King James Version of the Bible (KJV), the writer(s) could not decide if the woman would be the Levite's concubine or wife. In the first three sentences, the woman is referred to as his concubine twice, and the Levite is referred to as her husband. Both cannot be true because, if he is her husband, then she must be his wife. The woman is never referenced as the Levite's wife, therefore leaving the impression that she is his concubine. Nevertheless, this mislabeling is confusing and continues back and forth in different forms, throughout the story. So, as you read the story in its entirety in the KJV, be aware of this problem. The Concubine: Book of Judges 19:1-29.

The Concubine

Judges 19:1–27 (short story)

There was a certain Levite who took to him a concubine out of Bethlehem Judah. His concubine played the whore against him, and went away to her father's house. The Levite went after her, to speak friendly to her, and to bring her back. *When he arrived*: She invited him into her father's house, and when the father saw him, he rejoiced to meet him.... When the man began to leave, with his concubine, her father, said to him, stay another night, but the man would not stay and departed and as he traveled, the sun went down upon them in the land of Benjamin.... An old man looked up and saw the Levite, a wayfaring man, in the street. So he brought him into his house...and they washed their feet, and did eat and drink. As they were making their hearts merry, the men of the city surrounded the house and beat on the door, and spoke to the old man, saying: bring out the man that came into your house, that we may know (rape) him. Then the old man, went out to them, and said, do nothing so wickedly; seeing that this man has come into my house, do not this folly. Here is my daughter a maiden and his concubine; them I will bring out now, and humble yourselves with them, and do with them what seems good to you: but to this man do nothing. The men (surrounding the house) would not listen to him: so the Levite took his concubine, and brought her to them; and they knew her, and abused her all night until the morning. When the day began to spring, they let her go. The concubine in the dawning of the day, came and fell down at the door of the old man's house. When the Levite woke up the next morning, and opened the doors of the house, to go his way, he found the concubine dead at the door of the house, and her hands were upon the threshold....

About the Levite

The story of the concubine is not actually about the woman. It's about the Levite. This story focuses on the actions of a man who was identified as a Levite but not named. A certain Levite who followed after a woman he believed to have cheated on him (played the whore) to her father's house, probably because he had feelings for her. He stayed for days to "speak friendly to her," in hopes that she would come back with him. He entered into a stranger's house and became the original target of an angry mob of men who wanted to rape him sexually. He sacrificed his concubine to save himself and charged all twelve tribes of Israel to revenge his concubine's rape and death, which led to war against one of their own, the tribe of Benjamin.

Who were the Levites?

Levi was the third son born to Jacob with his first wife, Leah. The descendants of Levi were known as the Levites, the priestly tribe, and the thirteenth tribe. Aaron and his sons were Levites, chosen by God to be priest over all (twelve tribes) of Israel. The remaining Levites were not priests; nor could they become priests. They were given duties to assist the priest (Aaron and his sons) and maintain the tabernacle for all the Israelites.

Numbers 3:6–9

> Bring the tribe of Levi near, and present them before Aaron the priest, that they may minister to him… And you shall give the Levites to Aaron and to his sons: they are solely given to him out of the children of Israel.

THE SOLE PURPOSE OF TITHING

According to the scriptures, the sole purpose for tithing came about because of the Levites. In exchange for the work performed by the priest and the remaining Levites, they were to receive tithes from the twelve tribes of Israel as an inheritance from the Lord. Each of the twelve tribes was to give a tenth of its first-fruits, such as grains, fruits, and spices to the Levites. In return, the remaining Levites were to give a tenth (a heave offering) of the best of all they received (the Lord's portion) to the priest, Aaron and his sons.

Numbers 18:20–21

> The LORD spoke to Aaron, you shall have no inheritance in their land, neither shall you have any part among them: I am...your inheritance among the children of Israel. And, behold, I have given the children of Levi all the tenth in Israel for an inheritance, for their service...of the tabernacle of the congregation....

Numbers 18:28

> ...You shall offer a heave offering to the LORD of all your tithes, which you receive of the children of Israel; and you shall give the LORD'S heave offering to Aaron the priest.

Originally the remaining Levites were to serve only the priest, Aaron and his sons, which meant, when Aaron and his sons died, the priesthood would cease. There would be no priest to perform the animal sacrifices and blood rituals or carry the ark of the covenant from place to place. Then there would be no priest (Aaron and his sons) for the Levites to assist, no need to maintain the tabernacle, no need for tithing, and no forgiveness of sin following the death of Aaron's last living son.

ABOUT THE CONCUBINE

In telling the story of a woman being raped, the writer(s) captures your attention within one verse, with a vague statement, "they knew her, and abused her all the night until the morning," implying she was gang-raped, which were the intentions of the angry mob toward the Levite.

Rape all by itself is ugly. Why the writer(s) chose to dirty up the woman in the beginning of the story is unclear (although this happens to rape victims to this very day). The concubine was made out to be an unsympathetic character by saying "she played the whore." How unsympathetic the reader is toward the woman would depend on who the woman was. Biblically speaking, if the woman was the man's wife and she had sex with another man (played the whore), under the Old Testament law, she committed adultery and would have been worthy of death (not to be raped).

If the woman was only a concubine, she is a single woman. She may be called a wife, but she is only an instrument used for the purposes of having sex or bearing children and nothing more. For example, consider the story of Abram (Abraham) and his wife Sarai (Sarah) who gave her servant Hagar to her husband for the purpose of giving them a child, because she was barren and Abram had no heir. Hagar conceived and did give birth to a son named Ishmael.

Genesis 16:1–3

> Now Sarai Abram's wife…had an handmaid, an Egyptian, whose name was Hagar. And Sarai said to Abram…the LORD has restrained me from bearing…it may be that I may obtain children by her. And Abram listened to the voice of Sarai. And Sarai…took Hagar her maid…and gave her to her husband Abram to be his wife.

Genesis 16:15

> Hagar bare Abram a son: and Abram called his son's name… Ishmael.

According to the scriptures, the Lord God later blessed Sarah and Abraham, and Sarah conceived and gave birth to a son, whom they named Isaac. The scriptures tell us that Isaac inherited everything from his father and received the honor and blessing of continuing the bloodline as his son. However, Abraham's son Ishmael was considered the son of his concubine, and he only received gifts from his father and was sent away.

Genesis 25:5

> Abraham gave all that he had to Isaac. But to the sons of the concubines…Abraham gave gifts, and sent them away from Isaac his son…

Nevertheless, in this case, it should not matter whether the woman was his wife or his concubine, because she was a woman who was brutally raped and murdered.

Now, many may ask why didn't God protect the Levite and save the Concubine, as he protected and saved Lot, his wife and two daughters, who were the only survivors of God's wrath upon Sodom and Gomorrah? If God is omnipresent, all-knowing, and the Alpha and the Omega, where was God?

When the Levite forcibly threw his concubine out of the house, kicking and screaming, to an angry mob of vicious dirty and smelly men! Where was God?

When the angry mob ripped her clothes from her body! Where was God?

When the woman cried out no and begged them to stop! Where was God?

When they beat her with their fists! Where was God?

When they held her down! Where was God?

When they forced their lips upon hers! Where was God?

When they spread open her legs, forcing their penises inside her vagina! Where was God?

When they forced their penises in her mouth to be sucked dry! Where was God?

When they forcibly put their penises into her rectum! Where was God?

When they verbally abused her, calling her a slut and a whore! Where was God?

When the first man was raping her! Where was God?

When the second man was raping her! Where was God?

When the last man was raping her! Where was God?

When the concubine, one of God's chosen people died at the old man's door, from her injuries. Where was God? Where was God's Wrath!

CHAPTER 6

Dearly beloved, avenge not yourselves,
but rather give place to wrath: for it is written,
Vengeance is mine; I will repay, saith the Lord.
Romans 12:19

"WRATH: The emotional response to perceived wrong and injustice,
often translated: anger, indignation, vexation, and irritation."
Holman Bible Dictionary

"WRATH: God' anger is not capricious, spasmodic, or changing;
but constant and unchanging against sin, though wholly tempered
by His justice. Anger or wrath is an essential element of divine love,
and realization of it produces a wholesome fear of God."
Wycliffe Bible Encyclopedia

"WRATH: The wrath of God against all ungodliness and
Unrighteousness of men is plainly declared in scripture, and will
surely fall upon the children of disobedience."
Concise Bible Dictionary

"WRATH: 1. Strong, stern, or fierce anger; deeply resentful
indignation. 2. Vengeance or punishment as the conse-
quence of anger"
Webster's Encyclopedic Unabridged Dictionary

Why the Destruction?

MUCH OF THE PREACHING AND teaching throughout the Christian community is settled on these three facts: God hears the prayers and cries of the righteous; God will always provide a way of escape (out of danger) for the righteous in any situation; Lastly, the righteous will be saved from all damnation. In the book of Genesis, these are the same three things the writer(s) wanted us to know about God's wrath upon the people of Sodom and Gomorrah.

God's wrath is demonstrated throughout the Old Testament, against the wicked, ungodly, wrongdoers, non-believers, and the innocent. One of the most prominent acts of God's wrath upon the earth, second to the flood is Sodom and Gomorrah. The writer(s) summarized God's wrath, on Sodom and Gomorrah in just two sentences.

Genesis 19:24-25

> Then the LORD rained upon Sodom and upon Gomorrah brimstone and fire from the LORD out of heaven; he overthrew those cities, and all the plain, and all the inhabitants of the cities, and that which grew upon the ground.

Many Christians may believe that God destroyed Sodom and Gomorrah because of consensual same-sex relations among men. Until Christians and non-Christians have an understanding of why God destroyed Sodom and Gomorrah, they may continue to believe or accept what is often taught from the pulpit or within the Christian community.

There are actually two different reasons given for the destruction of Sodom and Gomorrah: the cries of the righteous and a lack of ten righteous souls.

THE CRIES OF THE RIGHTEOUS

The cries of the righteous, was how the story began, and was the basis for the destruction of Sodom and Gomorrah.

Genesis 18:20
> The LORD said, because the cry of Sodom and Gomorrah is great, and because their sin is very grievous; I will go down now, and see whether they have done altogether according to the cry of it, which came to me; and if not, I will know.

In the story, God did not actually go down to investigate, but sent two witnesses in the form of men/angels to Sodom.

Genesis 19:1
> There came two angels to Sodom…

What is not clear is why God destroyed Gomorrah, because no witnesses were sent to investigate, if the cries in Gomorrah were true. In Genesis 19:13, the reason given by God's witnesses for the destruction of Sodom and Gomorrah was "because the cry of *them*, is waxen great before the face of the LORD." The writer(s) did not make known the reason for the righteous crying out; however, one could conclude it involved rape. Now, what is interesting is who was crying out.

Genesis 19:12–13
> The men said to Lot: Are there any others here besides your, son-in-law, sons, or daughters? Bring them out: For we will destroy this place, because the cry of them is waxen great before the face of the LORD; and the LORD has sent us to destroy it.

Only four people were saved out of Sodom: Lot, his wife, and their two daughters. It is clear that Lot did not cry out because the witnesses were speaking to Lot and told him that they were going to destroy Sodom "because the cry of them is waxen great before the face of the LORD." They did not say to Lot that God heard his cries or prayers. The only other people who could have cried out were Lot's wife and daughter(s). Therefore, God destroyed Sodom and Gomorrah because of the cries of "them," women.

Ten Righteous Souls

When you analyze the scriptures closely, a different story emerges concerning the destruction of Sodom and Gomorrah. According to the scriptures, in Genesis 18:17, God was going to destroy Sodom and Gomorrah all along before the witnesses (went down to investigate the cry of the righteous) reached Sodom. God said, "Shall I hide from Abraham that thing which I do," which implied that God was going to do something. Then in Genesis 18:20, God made known to Abraham how egregious Sodom and Gomorrah was. What follows in Genesis 18:23–32 was Abraham bargaining with God to spare Sodom, if there was a minimum of ten righteous people found there.

Genesis 18:17
> The LORD said: shall I hide from Abraham that thing which I do…

Genesis 18:20
> The LORD said, because the cry of Sodom and Gomorrah is great, and because their sin is very grievous…

Genesis 18:23–32

> Abraham drew near, and said, will you destroy the righteous with the wicked? Peradventure there be fifty righteous people within the city... and the LORD said, if I find in Sodom fifty righteous people within the city, I will spare all for their sakes. Then Abraham said... Peradventure there shall lack five of the fifty righteous, will you destroy the city for a lack of five? Then the Lord said: If I find forty five, I will not destroy it.... Peradventure there shall be forty found there, and he said, I will not destroy it, if I find forty.... Peradventure if there is only thirty to be found there, and he said, I will not destroy it, if I find thirty there.... Peradventure there shall be twenty found there, and he said, I will not destroy it. Let not the Lord be angry, and I will speak yet again: Peradventure ten shall be found there, and he said, I will not destroy it if I find ten there.

Therefore, God was willing to act and going to act from the beginning. What other reason is there for Abraham to ask God if he was going to destroy the righteous with the wicked, if God was not bent on destroying something or someone? Leaving some Christians with the impression that God destroyed Sodom and Gomorrah because there were not ten righteous people within two cities. Now, if Sodom and Gomorrah was so sinful that God could not find ten righteous people, then why did God save Sodom and Gomorrah in the War of the Kings from their enemies through Abram (Abraham)?

THE WAR OF THE KINGS

Four kings went to war and prevailed against the five kings. Among the five kings were Sodom and Gomorrah. After the four kings prevailed, they took all that belonged to the five kings, including all the people, which included Abram's nephew, Lot. Abram and 318 men went in pursuit of the four kings and were successful. They returned with Lot, all his goods, and all the people, including those of Sodom and Gomorrah. After Abram returned, the king of Salem (priest of the most high God) blessed him, declaring that God had delivered the four kings into Abram's hands.

Therefore, this leaves some Christians with the belief that God saved Sodom and Gomorrah. Now, the question is: Why did God save Sodom and Gomorrah, from their enemies, which He believed were exceeding evil, to then later destroy them? If God is the Alpha and the Omega and omnipresent, why didn't God save only Lot and his possessions in the War of the Kings to prevent the suffering of others?

Genesis 14:11–12

> They took all the goods of Sodom and Gomorrah…and went their way. They took Lot, Abram's brother's son, who lived in Sodom, and his goods, and departed…

Genesis 14:14

> When Abram heard that Lot was taken captive, he armed his trained servants, born in his own house, three hundred and eighteen, and pursued them…

Genesis 14:16

> Then he brought back all the goods, and also brought back Lot and all his goods, the women, and all the people…

Genesis 14:18–23

> Then Melchizedek king of Salem (a priest)…said, blessed be Abram of the most high God, possessor of heaven and earth: and blessed be the most high God, which has delivered your enemies into your hand.

According to the scriptures, the city of Sodom did not consist of men alone. The very reason that Lot came to live in Sodom was because he along with Abram had too much wealth that they were both unable to live in the land of Canaan together with all the other Canaanites. Lot chose Sodom because it appeared pleasing to his eyes, not because of any history concerning men being raped. He came to Sodom with all his cattle, herdsmen, and tents when he separated from Abram.

When Abram saved Lot during the War of the Kings, there was no mention of Lot having a wife or children, even though women and other people were mentioned as being saved. Therefore, this leaves an impression that Lot met, married his wife, and had children while living in Sodom. Also both of Lot's daughters were married, which shows the people were going about their lives as normal. Surely some of Lot's herdsmen brought their wives or concubines with them when they settled in Sodom. The point here is: there were other women, and children living in Sodom. What the scriptures tell us about Sodom and Gomorrah is that only Lot, his wife, and two daughters were saved, meaning everyone else and all their possessions were left behind and destroyed.

What happened to the other women and children saved in the War of the Kings? They were clearly not counted among the righteous with Lot's wife and daughters because, if six additional righteous souls were found, then God would not have rained down fire and brimstone (burning sulfur) upon the bodies of the wicked like bombs, setting them ablaze to burn from the outside in, one man looking upon another while each one screams out in agonizing pain with the smell of burning flesh, homes, and trees permeating their airways, slowly suffocating them all while being conscious, until each one was turned into a pile of ashes.

Ask yourself: What did the women and children do? What did the animals do? What did every seed-bearing tree, shrub, or plant do that they were worthy to be destroyed? God once said they were all good.

Genesis 1:10–12

> God called the dry land Earth; and the gathering together of the waters he called Seas: and God saw that it was good. The earth brought forth grass, and herb yielding seed after his kind, and the tree yielding fruit after his kind: and God saw that it was good.

Genesis 1:25

> God made the beast of the earth after his kind, and cattle after their kind, and everything that creep upon the earth after his kind: and God saw that it was good.

Genesis 1:31

> God saw everything that he had made, and, behold, it was very good.

Some may believe that Sodom and Gomorrah was destroyed because of the cries of the righteous, women, or there were not ten righteous people found within two cities. However, no one should believe that Sodom and Gomorrah was about consensual same-sex relations, because it is not. It's about rape.

CHAPTER 7

God's Wrath

———

He that believeth on the Son has everlasting life:
and he that believeth not the Son shall not see life;
but the wrath of God abideth on him.
John 3:36

WHEN IT COMES TO THE New Testament, the story of Sodom and Gomorrah was used mainly as a comparison or an example of God's wrath against any and every one for not believing in the message or teachings of God and Christ. For example,

The Gospel of Matthew

Matthew 11:20-24

Then began he to upbraid the cities wherein most of his mighty works were done, because they repented not... **"And you, Capernaum, which are exalted to heaven, shall be brought down to hell: for if the mighty works, which have been done in you, had been done in Sodom, it would have remained until this day. But I say to you, that it shall be more** tolerable for the land of Sodom in the day of judgment, than for you."

The Gospel of Mark

Mark 6:11–12
> **Whosoever shall not receive you, nor hear you, when you depart…shake off the dust under your feet for a testimony against them. Verily I say to you, it shall be more tolerable for Sodom and Gomorrha in the day of judgment, than for that city.** And they went out, and preached that men should repent.

The Book of 2 Peter

2 Peter 2:6
> Then turning the cities of Sodom and Gomorrha into ashes condemned them with an overthrow, making them an ensample to those that after should live ungodly.

THE BOOK OF JUDE

The book of Jude goes one step further, which causes confusion because it is the only book in the New Testament that tries to explain what Sodom and Gomorrah was all about, but it misses the mark completely.

Jude is one of the shortest books in the entire Bible with only one chapter containing twenty-five verses. It is not clear whether Jude is the writer. In fact, theologians have written that it is probably Jude, meaning they don't know. The purpose of the book of Jude is to challenge those who do not believe as they do or who do not continue to believe as they do. It is an attempt to smear men as ungodly, for not accepting the Christian teachings of God and Christ.

Jude 1:3–4

> Beloved, when I gave all diligence to write to you of the common salvation, it was needful for me to write to you, and exhort you that you should earnestly contend for the faith which was once delivered to the saints. For there are certain men crept in unawares, who were before of old ordained... ungodly men, turning the grace of our God into lasciviousness, and denying the only Lord God, and our Lord Jesus Christ.

Jude's fantastic stories of angels and God's wrath in the following scriptures are to scare the believer(s) into keeping the faith. They are not supported by any other scriptures in the entire Bible, and appear to have been made up out of thin air. For example:

Jude 1:6

> The angels which kept not their first estate, but left their own habitation, he has reserved in everlasting chains under darkness to the judgment of the great day.

Jude 1:9

> Yet Michael the archangel, when contending with the devil he disputed about the body of Moses, dare not bring against him a railing accusation, but said, The Lord rebuke you.

Jude 1:14-15

> Enoch also, the seventh from Adam, prophesied of these, saying, Behold, the Lord cometh with ten thousands of his saints, To execute judgment upon all, and to convince all that are ungodly among them of all their ungodly deeds which they have ungodly committed, and of all their hard speeches which ungodly sinners have spoken against him.

What stands out in the book of Jude is his utter lack of understanding of what the story of Sodom and Gomorrah was actually about.

Jude 1:7

> Even as Sodom and Gomorrha, and the cities about them in like manner, giving themselves over to fornication, and going after strange flesh, set forth an example of suffering the vengeance of eternal fire.

Many in the Christian community may believe and cite Jude's assertion that Sodom and Gomorrah was about fornication and "going after strange flesh" because it is in the Bible, although they could read the story of Sodom and Gomorrah for themselves and know that it's not. Now what is meant by "going after strange flesh" would depend upon the reader's interpretation. Some may say bestiality, others may say something else.

By definition, "fornication" means consenting sex between individuals who are not married. Therefore, single men and women who have consensual same-sex relations with a partner who is not married are fornicators, just like single men and women who have consensual sex with a partner of the opposite sex who are not married. Many

Christians or non-Christians read the book of Jude, and walk away with the perception that having consensual sex with another person, who is not married, is wrong and worthy of God's wrath, which is eternal fire or hell. Biblically speaking, God was not against David for loving Jonathan. Likewise, God is not against a man having sex with a woman. A concubine is an unmarried woman. Remember, Abraham, Jacob, David, and Solomon were all married with more than one wife, and all had concubines. It is not written that they committed adultery (with the one exception of David and Bathsheba's relationship because she was married to another man), and God was with them, and they were not destroyed. So, why would God be against any man or woman having consensual sex with anyone else?

Jude is wrong. His lies or misunderstanding of the truth about Sodom and Gomorrah is one of the reasons for abstinence (no sex until marriage). The main reason why abstinence is preached and taught throughout the Christian community is because Paul was against fornication, a man and a woman having consensual sex outside of marriage.

1 Corinthians 7:1–2

> Now concerning the things you wrote to me: It is good for a man not to touch a woman. Nevertheless, to avoid fornication, let every man have his own wife, and let every woman have her own husband.

Ask yourself: Why couldn't Jude simply write that Sodom and Gomorrah was about men wanting to rape or covet other men, or an attempted gang rape? One would think Jude would be knowledgeable about the facts of Sodom and Gomorrah, if he was inspired by

God. However, Jude is just a man whose lies and interpretations of the facts concerning Sodom and Gomorrah opens the door to all manner of misconceptions about rape, same-sex relations (to be specific), fornication, and bestiality.

CHAPTER 8

SODOMITE

———

WHEN YOU SEARCH BIBLICAL REFERENCE materials such as the *Wycliffe Bible Encyclopedia* and the *Holman Bible Dictionary* for additional information concerning Sodom and Gomorrah, you are quickly steered to the belief that Sodom and Gomorrah is about consensual same-sex relations among men or something else.

THE WYCLIFFE BIBLE ENCYCLOPEDIA

When you search for Sodom and Gomorrah in the *Wycliffe Bible Encyclopedia*, it is two separate searches. When you search the name "Sodom," what you will find is vague information about the people and their destruction. Then you are quickly steered to the word "sodomite."

SODOM

* "Lot chose this area for his residence when he broke company with Abraham, even though Sodom was a very

wicked city (Gen 13:1-13)... Later it and several other cities of the plain were destroyed by fire and brimstone as a judgment of God, because of their abject immorality (**see Sodomite**)."

<u>SODOMITE</u>

* "One who practiced that unnatural sexual perversion which characterized ancient Sodom, namely, carnal copulation between male persons (Gen. 19:5)."

To be clear, the *Wycliffe Bible Encyclopedia* appears to be saying that God destroyed Sodom and Gomorrah along with other cities because of their abject immorality, namely carnal copulation between male persons. Implying that what took place among the men of Sodom and Gomorrah was consensual same-sex relations, which is fornication.

———◆———

When you search for the name "Gomorrah," this is what you will find.

<u>GOMORRAH</u>

* "The twin cities of Sodom and Gomorrah were most intimately associated as cities of gross sin (Gen 18:20; Mt 10:15). Condemnation of Sodom is shared by the city of Gomorrah (Gen 18:20; II Peter 2:6; Jude 7)."

The only information concerning Gomorrah includes Sodom; therefore, Gomorrah must also be about consensual same-sex relations, which is fornication.

THE HOLMAN BIBLE DICTIONARY

When you search the *Holman Bible Dictionary* for the name "Sodom and Gomorrah" for addition information, what you will find is a very short description of the events concerning their destruction. Then the reader is steered toward the word "sodomy."

SODOM AND GOMORRAH

* "Sodom and Gomorrah were renowned for their wickedness. Despite Abraham's successful plea not even ten righteous men could be found in Sodom, and the cities were judged by the Lord, then destroyed by brimstone and fire."
* "The unnatural lusts of the men of Sodom (Gen. 19:4-8; Jude 7) have given us the modern term sodomy…"

The *Holman Bible Dictionary* presents what appears to be a vague misrepresentation of the truth about the people of Sodom and Gomorrah and their destruction. There are four things which need to be addressed in order to have a clear understanding of what the truth really is.

The first thing is: Sodom and Gomorrah was not famous in the Bible for their wickedness prior to their destruction. Remember the War of the Kings where God saved Sodom and Gomorrah through Abram and his men. At that time there was no mention of men coveting (raping) or wanting to covet (rape) other men.

The second thing is: The scriptures actually tell us that Sodom and Gomorrah was destroyed because of the cries of women (based on God's two witnesses sent to Sodom).

The third thing is: It is not true that the destruction came about because there were not "ten righteous <u>men</u>" found in Sodom. In fact, Abraham argued on behalf of the righteous. He did not specify men or women. The question that Abraham asked of God in Genesis 18:23 was: "Will you destroy the righteous with the wicked?" Therefore women were included among the righteous because Lot's wife and daughters were saved.

Why write these things if they can be proven in scriptures to not be true? One reason perhaps is to shape the readers perception about the men of Sodom and Gomorrah who were inherently evil, wicked, and unrighteous and then to relate that perception to actual men today in or desiring a same-sex relationship. What supports this view is the fourth and final thing, where the "modern term sodomy" is introduced in the second paragraph.

When you search for the word "sodomy," it's not in the dictionary. However, what you will find is the word "sodomite," which simply means a person who practices sodomy.

SODOMITE

* "Originally a citizen of the town of Sodom... The term came to mean a male who has sexual relations with another male.

The wickedness of Sodom became proverbial (see Gen. 19:1-11). See Homosexuality; Sex."

Therefore, what the *Holman Bible Dictionary* appears to be saying about Sodom and Gomorrah was this: the unnatural lusts of the men of Sodom have given us the modern term "sodomy," which means a male who has sexual relations with another male. Also, it implies that what took place in Sodom and Gomorrah was not rape, but men having consensual same-sex relations, which is fornication. Now the word "sodomite" steers you to "see homosexuality." When you search for the word "homosexuality," this is what you will find.

HOMOSEXUALITY

* "Biblical references to homosexuality are relatively few. Genesis 19:1-11 tells the story of an attempted homosexual gang rape at the house of Lot by the wicked men of Sodom."

Now, it is absolutely clear that the *Holman Bible Dictionary* knew Sodom and Gomorrah was about rape all along. Why the deception?

The *Holman Bible Dictionary* and the *Wycliffe Bible Encyclopedia* appear to be outright manipulating, deceiving, and lying to their readers on the topic of Sodom and Gomorrah. It takes determination and effort on their part to steer their readers to the belief that Sodom and Gomorrah was about consensual same-sex relations instead of rape. It would appear the only purpose for the deception is for you (the reader) to believe or accept that Sodom and Gomorrah is about consensual same-sex relations and that consensual same-sex relations are wrong, inherently evil, wicked, and unrighteous.

THE WORDS SODOMY AND SODOMITE

The words "sodomy" and "sodomite" comes directly from the Bible, particularly the story of Sodom and Gomorrah in the book of Genesis. Sodom was the city where all the evil men surrounded Lot's house and demanded that he send out the two witnesses to be raped. This essentially is the story of Sodom and Gomorrah, which produced the words "sodomy" and "sodomite."

The *Holman Bible Dictionary* and the *Wycliffe Bible Encyclopedia* both cite the terms "sodomy" or "sodomite" to define the actions of the men of Sodom. When you search non-biblical dictionaries and reference materials for the words "sodomy" or "sodomite," here are a few examples of what you will find:

"Sodomy: 1. an offensive term for anal intercourse
2. an offensive term for sexual intercourse with an animal."
Encarta ® World English Dictionary

"Sodomite: an offensive term for somebody who practices anal intercourse."
Encarta ® World English Dictionary

"Sodomy: Is generally anal or oral sex between people or sexual activity between a person and a non-human animal (bestiality), but may also mean any non-procreative sexual activity."
https://en.wikipedia.org/wiki/sodomy_law

"Sodomite: A person who practice sodomy."
https://en.wikipedia.org/wiki/sodomy_law

———

"Sodomy: 1. Anal or oral copulation with a member of the opposite sex. 2. Copulation with a member of the same sex. 3. Bestiality"
Webster's Encyclopedic Unabridged Dictionary

"Sodomite: 1. an inhabitant of Sodom. 2. A person who engages in Sodomy."
Webster's Encyclopedic Unabridged Dictionary

Again, it should be absolutely clear that what took place in Sodom was not fornication or bestiality. In fact, the entire story of Sodom and Gomorrah never mentions or names any beast or animal. Therefore, using the words "sodomy" or "sodomite" to describe the actions of the men of Sodom or any man is wrong. To be clear, the *Holman Bible Dictionary* and *Wycliffe Bible Encyclopedia* do not say explicitly that Sodom and Gomorrah had anything to do with bestiality. However, taking a closer look at the *Holman Bible Dictionary* under "Sodom and Gomorrah" and the *Wycliffe*

Bible Encyclopedia under "Gomorrah," and "Sodom/Sodomite," they both cite the word "unnatural" and Jude 7. Why?

SODOM AND GOMORRAH
Holman Bible Dictionary

* "The **unnatural** lusts of the men of Sodom **(**Gen. 19:4-8; **Jude 7)** have given us the modern term sodomy…"

GOMORRAH
Wycliffe Bible Encyclopedia

* "The twin cities of Sodom and Gomorrah were most intimately associated as cities of gross sin (Gen 18:20; Mt 10:15). Condemnation of Sodom is shared by the city of Gomorrah (Gen 18:20; II Peter 2:6; **Jude 7**)."

SODOM/SODOMITE
Wycliffe Bible Encyclopedia

* "Later it and several other cities of the plain were destroyed by fire and brimstone as a judgment of God, because of their abject immorality. (see Sodomite)."
* "One who practiced that **unnatural** sexual perversion which characterized ancient Sodom, namely, carnal copulation between male persons"

Jude 1:7

> "Even as Sodom and Gomorrha, and the cities about them in
> like manner, giving themselves over to fornication, and going
> after strange flesh, are set forth for an example, suffering the
> vengeance of eternal fire."

When you take a closer look at Jude 7, it mentions two specific
things about the men of Sodom and Gomorrah: They were "giving themselves over to fornication," and "going after strange flesh."
Based on the definition of the word sodomy, (using a non-biblical
dictionary such as *Webster's Encyclopedic Unabridged Dictionary* – noted
earlier) bestiality could only be attributed to something else, other
than fornication, which is "going after strange flesh." If not, why cite
Jude 7 at all, which is a total lie.

The Word Sodomite in the Bible

The words "sodomy" and "sodomite" have always been associated with the Bible, based on the city of Sodom. It is commonly accepted in the Christian community that men in a same-sex relationship are sometimes referred to as sodomites, especially, when referencing the Bible. The word "sodomy" does not appear in the King James Version of the Bible. However, the word "sodomite" is mentioned once in Deuteronomy, and the word "sodomites" is mentioned four times within First and Second Kings.

Deuteronomy 23:17-18

> There shall be no whore of the daughters of Israel, nor a sodomite of the sons of Israel. You shall not bring the hire of a whore, or the price of a dog, into the house of the LORD your God for any vow: both are an abomination to the LORD thy God.

1 Kings 14:24

> There were also sodomites in the land: and they did according to all the abominations of the nations which the LORD cast out before the children of Israel.

1 Kings 15:12

> He took +away the sodomites out of the land, and removed all the idols that his fathers had made.

1 Kings 22:46

> The remnant of the sodomites, which remained in the days of his father Asa, he took out of the land.

2 Kings 23:7
> He tore down the houses of the sodomites that were by the house of the LORD…

In the book of Deuteronomy, the words "whore" and "sodomite" were both used as labels to define certain men and women of Israel as prostitutes. Therefore, First and Second Kings must also be referring to Sodomites as prostitutes.

> **"Prostitute:** 1. somebody paid for sexual intercourse: somebody who is paid to provide sexual intercourse or other sex acts"
> *Encarta ® World English Dictionary*

A prostitute is someone who has consensual sex with men or women for a fee. It should be clear from the scriptures, that they were not referring to sex with animals (bestiality) because of the phrases "you shall not bring the hire of a whore, or the price of a dog" refers to money earned (via prostitution) and animals do not pay for sex. The *Holman Bible Dictionary*, the *Wycliffe Bible Encyclopedia*, and the non-biblical reference materials (listed earlier) do not define the words "sodomy" or "sodomite" as being related to prostitution. The only reason to mention bestiality within the definition is for you, the reader, to believe or accept that consensual same-sex relations are wrong, inherently evil, wicked, and unrighteous. In addition, it demonizes men and women in or desiring a same-sex relationship or marriage today.

Therefore, based on the King James Version of the Bible, the definitions for the words "sodomy" and "sodomites" (with the exception of the *Encarta World English Dictionary*) appear to be built on lies and not on any story or books of the Bible and should be seen as offensive, ignorant, malicious, and hateful.

Rape is a very important subject for the Bible to touch on, regardless of how fantastic the stories are. When you read the stories of Sodom and Gomorrah and The Concubine, they are clearly not about fornication (consensual sex) or bestiality (sex with animals). They are about rape. So, why are these stories not translated correctly in the Christian community and beyond, as being about rape?

The pen is mightier
than the sword.

—*Sir Edward Bulwer-Lytton*

CHAPTER 9

ABOUT PAUL

———

There is no greater opponent against same-sex relations than Paul (formerly known as Saul, as described in the book of Acts) in the entire Bible. Paul began his letter to the Romans talking disparagingly about "them," meaning men and women in or desiring a same-sex relationship. After making known God's vengeance toward his creation, Paul expressed his views concerning same-sex relations. Following his introduction and salutations, Paul wrote the following:

Romans 1:18, 24–27 (short

> For the wrath of God is revealed from heaven against all ungodliness and unrighteousness of men... Wherefore God also gave them up to uncleanness through the lusts of their own hearts, to dishonor their own bodies between themselves: Who changed the truth of God into a lie, and worshipped and served the creature more than the Creator, who is blessed for ever. Amen. For this cause God gave them up to vile affections: for even their women did change the natural use into that which is against nature: likewise also the men, leaving the natural use of the woman, burned in their lust

one toward another; men with men working that which is unseemly, and receiving in themselves that recompense of their error which was meet.

What Paul wrote thus far in his first chapter to the Romans, he seemed to be using men and women in a same-sex relationship to project his beliefs that same-sex relations is deviant sexual behavior. In the entire Bible, there is nothing mentioned about women wanting women sexually, nor any deviant sexual behavior concerning woman. This was not the case with the men of Sodom. That's why Paul masterfully included women in verse 26, to make it solely about same-sex relations and not just an issue with men.

Romans 1:26
> For this cause God gave them up to vile affections: for even their women did change the natural use into that which is against nature:

When you look at verse 26, Paul is referring to women in a same-sex relationship in around about way. Notice, Paul does not use the word "lust" in relation to the women. Now when you look just at the first half of verse 27, Paul used the word "lust" to describe the interactions among men in a same-sex relationship. In the second half of verse 27, Paul purposely linked men who have same-sex relations to the men of Sodom and Gomorrah.

Romans 1:27 (first half)
> Likewise also the men, leaving the natural use of the woman, burned in their lust one toward another;

Romans 1:27 (second half)

Men with men working that which is unseemly and receiving the recompense of their error which was appropriate.

Paul began in Romans 1:18, making mention of God's wrath being revealed from heaven on the unrighteous. There is no other story in the entire Bible, where men wanted or desired other men sexually ("working that which is unseemly"), and received an appropriate punishment for their actions ("receiving the recompense of their error which was appropriate"), other than Sodom and Gomorrah. It seems as though Paul wants you, the reader, to be reminded of deviant sexual behavior whenever you think of men in or desiring a same-sex relationship. Besides that, there is no other reason why the second half of verse 27 would be included, except to tie men who have same-sex relations to deviant sexual behavior. Paul went even further in verses 28 through 32, projecting all deviant and ill behavior he could think of onto men and women in or desiring a same-sex relationship.

Romans 1:28-32

Even as they did not like to retain God in their knowledge, God gave them over to a reprobate mind, to do those things which are not convenient; Being filled with all unrighteousness, fornication, wickedness, covetousness, maliciousness; full of envy, murder, debate, deceit, malignity; whisperers, Backbiters, haters of God, despiteful, proud, boasters, inventors of evil things, disobedient to parents, Without understanding, covenantbreakers, without natural affection, implacable, unmerciful: Who knowing the judgment of God, that they which commit such things are worthy of death, not only do the same, but have pleasure in them that do them.

Paul was not saying that God wanted him to say to men and women in or desiring a same-sex relationship, "stop or change your behavior." Paul was speaking for God or as God in condemning consensual same-sex relations. At the same time, Paul wants Christians to accept or believe that his stance against same-sex relations was not his view, but God's.

Romans 1:24

> **God also gave them up to uncleanness** through the lusts of their own hearts, to dishonor their own bodies between themselves...

Romans 1:26

> **God gave them up to vile affections:** for even their women did change the natural use into that which is against nature: And likewise also the men...

Romans 1:28

> **God gave them over to a reprobate mind**, to do those things which are not convenient; being filled with all unrighteousness, fornication, wickedness, covetousness...

To say that God "gave them up" is to say that God's back is turned away from men and women who have same-sex relations or God wants nothing to do with men and women who have same-sex relations. The problem with Paul's assertions is two things: The first thing is: it defeats God's capacity for forgiveness, which all Christians rely on. The second and most important thing is: God's love for David. Remember, God made David king over His chosen people, after David made a "Covenant of Love" with another man, Jonathan. So, under what authority is Paul's pronouncement that God gave "them" up or God is against "them" warranted? Ask yourself: How is it that Paul would know that God gave "them" up and why? Did he ask God about "them?" Did God appear in a dream to tell Paul about "them?" Perhaps, God just spoke to Paul in the cool of the day and said, "I, God, have given up on men and women in a same-sex relationship because of their uncleanness, vile affections, and reprobate minds." It doesn't make sense, and it's not true. Now ask yourself: Why would God say anything to Paul about sex, unless he had a problem?

PAUL'S PROBLEM

You can surmise from Paul's own writings that he indeed had a problem with lust, which he dealt with deceptively by blaming his own actions on sin, the law, and therefore, God. Paul gave Christians and non-Christians a look into his soul where they can examine how he dealt with his own issues with sin, in Romans (chapters 7, verses: 7–25). Paul wrote in detail concerning his conviction, his rationale for his own actions, his justification for the law (which brought his sin to the light), and how he chose to overcome his problem on his road to redemption.

Now, in order to understand Paul and get a clearer picture of what he is saying about his problem, it is important to analyze his writings as it relates to "his sin" and "the law," separately. The reason for this is Paul's writing skills were unique and somewhat difficult to follow. In one sentence, Paul would say several different things, at times unrelated, adding a little truth to capture your attention away from the bold lie that he wanted you to accept or believe. For example, Paul wrote about his problem with lust, this way.

Romans 7:7
    …I had not known sin, but by the law: for I had not known lust, except the law had said: You shall not covet.

When you pick apart what Paul is saying about his problem in verse 7, phrase by phrase, he is saying four different things. The first three could all be true, however, the fourth thing is the lie he wants you to accept or believe. For example:

1. **I had not known sin, but by the law:** Paul recognized that his sin was because of the law. The law brought Paul sin (wrongdoing) to the light.
2. I had not known sin, but by the law: **for I had not known lust:** Paul defined his sin as "lust."
3. For I had not known lust, **except the law had said: You Shall Not Covet:** Paul equated his "lust" to the commandment, You Shall Not Covet.
4. **Except the law had said, You shall not covet:** Here is the lie! You Shall Not Covet is a commandment and not a law. Paul wants you to accept or believe that the commandment, You Shall Not Covet, is under the law when, in fact, the law(s) and the commandment(s) are two separate things, and nowhere in the law does it say, "You Shall Not Covet." Paul clearly acknowledged this fact, later, in verse 12.

Romans 7:12

Wherefore the law is holy, and the commandment holy, and just, and good.

Therefore, in order to layout a clear and precise pattern of Paul's problem and how he dealt with it, it is necessary to analyze his writings on "his sin" and "the law" from two separate perspectives. Then bring them together for a completed analysis about Paul.

Now, to clearly appreciate what Paul is saying about his problem, you must focus on the words "sin" and "law."

Romans 7:7–25

...I had not known sin, but by the law: for I had not known lust, except the law had said: You shall not covet. But sin, taking occasion by the commandment, worked in me all manner of concupiscence. For without the law sin was dead. For I was alive without the law once: but when the commandment came, sin revived, and I died. And the commandment, which was ordained to life, I found to be to death. For sin, taking occasion by the commandment, deceived me, and by it slew me. Wherefore the law is holy, and the commandment holy, and just, and good. Was then that which is good made death to me? God forbid. But sin, that it might appear sin, working death in me by that which is good; that sin by the commandment might become exceeding sinful. For we know that the law is spiritual: but I am carnal, sold under sin. For that which I do, I allow not: for what I would, that do I not; but what I hate, that do I. If then I do that which I would not, I consent to the law that it is good. Now then it is no more I that do it, but sin that dwelleth in me. For I know that in me (that is, in my flesh,) dwelleth no good thing: for to will is present with me; but how to perform that which is good, I find not. For the good that I would, I do not: but the evil which I would not, that I do. Now if I do that I would not, it is no more I that do it, but sin that dwelleth in me. I find then a law, that, when I would do good, evil is present with me. For I delight in the law of God after the inward man: But I see another law in my members, warring against the law of my mind, and bringing me into captivity to the law of sin which is in my members. O wretched man that I am! who shall deliver me from the body of this death? I thank

God through Jesus Christ our Lord. So then with the mind I myself serve the law of God; but with the flesh the law of sin.

Paul's Perspective on His Sin

Paul's perspective on his sin was to paint himself as a victim, while blaming his own actions on sin and God. He defined his sin by making a direct link between God's commandment, You Shall Not Covet and lust.

Romans 7:7

...I had not known sin, but by the law: for I had not known lust, except the law had said: You shall not covet.

Now remember the commandment, You Shall Not Covet, means to take by force wrongfully, what belongs to someone else, also known as rape. This commandment has two elements:

1. Property: meaning to take by force property that belongs to someone else, which is deviant behavior.
2. Lust: meaning to take by force sexually what belongs to someone else, which is deviant sexual behavior.

Paul was talking about the second element of the commandment.

Exodus 20:17

You shall not covet thy neighbor's house: You shall not covet thy neighbor's wife, nor his manservant, nor his maidservant, nor his ox, nor his ass, nor any thing that is thy neighbor's.

(First part)

You shall not covet thy neighbor's house.

(Second part)

> You shall not covet thy neighbor's wife, nor his manser-
> vant, nor his maidservant, nor his ox, nor his ass.

When you analyze Paul's own writings, it is clear that his sin was coveting, which he defined as lust, the same lust he projected onto men in a same-sex relationship, which made it sexual. He linked this same lust to the men of Sodom, who were rapists, which made it deviant behavior. Therefore, Paul clearly made his sin of coveting about deviant sexual behavior. Ask yourself: How can someone covet his neighbor's wife, manservant, maidservant, ox, or ass sexually, and it not be rape?

Paul gives us insight into how entrenched coveting was for him in verse 8, when he used the phrase "worked in me all manner of concupiscence." (For clarity, the word "concupiscence" means lust.) In other words, Paul was saying that sin produced in him all manner of covetous desire (lust).

Romans 7:8

> But sin, taking occasion by the commandment, worked in
> me all manner of concupiscence. For without the law sin was
> dead.

Romans 7:11

> For sin, taking occasion by the commandment, deceived me,
> and by it slew me.

Paul seemed to imply that his every covetous desire was because of sin. What is strange is how he used the word sin, in verses 8 and 11, as though he was talking about another person or entity other than himself. At the same time, he was painting himself as a victim, when he implied that "sin" produced in him all manner of covetous desire and deceived him. Paul went even further, in verses 14 through 16, when he acknowledged his sinful nature.

Romans 7:14-16

For we know that the law is spiritual: but I am carnal, sold under sin. For that which I do, I allow not: for what I would, that do I not; but what I hate, that do I. If then, I do that which I would not, I consent to the law that it is good.

When you analyze closely what Paul was saying, he appeared to be crying out in agony over his sin of coveting, as though he could not stop himself, when he said, "For that which I do, I allow not: for what I would, that do I not; but what I hate, that I do." He is clearly expressing himself as one who had hit rock bottom when he acknowledged his condition as "carnal" and stated how far gone he was when he referred to himself as being "sold under sin," giving the impression that his sin of coveting was an addiction.

Now momentarily consider an alcoholic, a person who drinks all the time and way too much. This person may not understand why he or she continues to drink. Even though drinking may give the person a momentary high, afterward he or she becomes sick and depressed, and the cycle starts all over again. Nevertheless, for an alcoholic to overcome his or her problem, he or she must take a minimum of four basic steps to heart:

1. Acknowledge he or she has a problem.
2. Take responsibility for his or her actions.

3. Want to stop.
4. Seek help.

Acknowledge the problem

...I had not known sin, but by the law: for I had not known lust, except the law had said: You shall not covet.

Take Responsibility

Paul seemed to have acknowledged his sin of coveting. However, Paul taking responsibility for his own actions was another issue. In an early assessment Paul blamed his own actions on sin in verses 8 and 11. Further into chapter 7, Paul was again blaming his own actions on sin.

Romans 7:17–20

Now then it is no more I that do it, but sin that dwelleth in me. For I know that in me (that is, in my flesh,) dwelleth no good thing: for to will is present with me; but how to perform that which is good, I find not. For the good that I would, I do not: but the evil which I would not, that I do. Now if I do that I would not, it is no more I that do it, but sin that dwelleth in me.

When you analyze closely Paul's rationale of his own action(s), his mental stability appears unstable. Paul clearly rejected the fact that he was responsible for his own "evil" actions of coveting. Instead he blamed his own actions on sin, as though he was possessed, when he said, "If I do that I would not, it is no more I that do it, but sin that dwelleth in me." Therefore, Paul was not acknowledging his sin of coveting as it related to his own actions. He was acknowledging what was being done to him by "sin," as though he was a victim. Using, the devil made me do it, as a form of defense.

Want to Stop

Paul began his letter to the Romans saying he was a servant of Jesus Christ (1:1) and that Jesus was declared to be the Son of God with power (1:4). Then in chapter 15, Paul openly acknowledged that he was a minister of Jesus Christ: to minister the gospel of God to the Gentiles.

Romans 15:15-16

Nevertheless, brethren, I have written more boldly to you in some sort, as putting you in mind, because of the grace that is given to me of God, that I should be the minister of Jesus Christ to the Gentiles, ministering the gospel of God.

Now let's just accept as fact, that Paul was possessed by sin, which caused him to do wrong (covet men, women, children, or animals). It is clear, Paul knew and acknowledged that he was possessed by sin (which was contrary to God and Jesus), because he tells us. However, if Paul was a servant and a minister of Jesus Christ, then he should have known that Jesus was a healer of the sick, possessed, and the mentally unstable.

Matthew 4:23–24

Jesus went about all Galilee, teaching in their synagogues, and preaching the gospel of the kingdom, and healing all manner of sickness and all manner of disease among the people. His fame went throughout all Syria: and they brought all the people with diseases and torments, those which were possessed with devils, those which were lunatic, and those that had the palsy; and he healed them.

Then he should have also known that Jesus established the twelve apostles (which Paul later claimed to be one) and gave them the power to do the same, heal the sick, raise the dead and cast out demons.

Mark 6:7

Jesus called the twelve apostles, and began to send them out two by two; and gave them power over unclean spirits...

Mark 6:12

They went out, and preached that men should repent and they cast out many devils, and anointed with oil many that were sick, and healed them.

If Paul truly believed he was possessed with evil, then one or more of the apostles could have healed him because he knew and met them all. In fact, they worked together to settle a dispute concerning circumcision.

Acts 15:1–2

Certain men taught the brethren, saying, except you be circumcised after the manner of Moses, you cannot be saved.... Paul and Barnabas had no small dissension...with them, they determined that Paul and Barnabas, and certain others should go up to Jerusalem to the apostles and elders about this question...

Acts 15:22

Then pleased...the apostles and elders, with the whole church, to send chosen men of their own company to Antioch with Paul and Barnabas...

Now just imagine what two or three apostles could have done in the name of Jesus, if they had known about Paul's problem. They could have laid hands on him or outstretched their hands toward him and prayed for healing on his behalf. If Paul wanted to stop, why didn't he seek healing from the apostles? Then again, the scriptures tell us in the book of Acts, that Paul himself performed outstanding miracles and healed others, just like Jesus.

Acts 14:8–11

> There sat a certain man being a cripple from his mother's womb, who never had walked: The same heard Paul speak. Paul who perceived that the man had faith to be healed, said with a loud voice stand upright on thy feet and he leaped and walked. When the people saw what Paul had done, they lifted up their voices and said: The gods have come down to us in the likeness of men.

Acts 16:16–18

> A certain damsel possessed with a spirit of divination which brought her masters much gain by telling the future (fortune teller): She followed Paul and those with him crying out and saying: These men are the servants of the most high God, which show us the way of salvation. This she did many days. Then Paul, being grieved, turned and said to the spirit, I command you in the name of Jesus Christ to come out of her. He (the spirit) came out that same hour.

Jesus said in Matthew 17:20, **If you have faith the size of a grain of mustard seed, you shall say to this mountain, move from here to there, and it shall move.** Surely, Paul's faith was greater than that of a mustard seed. So, why didn't he heal himself? Remember, Paul said sin produced in him all manner of covetous desire, this would include both elements of the command-ment, property and lust, making his actions far worse than the men of Sodom. Therefore, the only conclusion is, Paul did not want to stop, because if he did, he would have been healed.

Seek Help

Paul wrote in his second letter to the Corinthians that he sought help from the Lord (God) to take away the thorn in his flesh. He never mentioned specifically what his thorn in the flesh was. However, he seemed to know that the thorn in his flesh came from Satan (verse 7) and why (verse 1–6).

2 Corinthians 12:7-9

Lest I should be exalted above measure through the abun-dance of revelations, there was given to me a thorn in the flesh, the messenger of Satan to buffet me, lest I should be exalted above measure. For this thing I sought the Lord three times, that it might depart from me. And he said to me: **My grace is sufficient for you: for my strength is made perfect in weakness.** Most gladly therefore will I rather glory in my infirmities, that the power of Christ may rest upon me.

"**Revelation:** 1. information revealed: information that is newly disclosed, especially surprising, or valuable 2. sur-prising thing: a surprisingly good or valuable experience 3. disclosure: the revealing of something previously hidden

or secret 4. Christianity demonstration of divine will: a showing or revealing of what is believed to be divine will or truth"
Encarta ® World English Dictionary

To be clear, Paul a minister of Jesus Christ is saying that he was given "a thorn in the flesh," by Satan to torture him, because of his "revelations." So, What was Paul's revelations?

2 Corinthians 12:1-6

It is not expedient for me to glory. I will come to visions and revelations of the Lord. I knew a man in Christ more than fourteen years ago, (whether in the body, I cannot tell; or whether out of the body, I cannot tell: God knows). He was caught up to the third heaven and I knew such a man (whether in the body, or out of the body, I cannot tell: God knows). He was caught up into paradise and heard unspeakable words, which it is not lawful for a man to utter. In this man will I glory. Yet in myself I will not glory, except in my infirmities. Although, I would desire to glory, I shall not be a fool, for I will say the truth, but for now I will hold my tongue, lest any man should think of me above that which he see me to be, or that he hear of me.

When you analyze what Paul called his "revelations," he makes absolutely no sense. He is writing as though he was a witness to this man he knew fourteen years earlier, who ascended into a third heaven or paradise. Paul repeated himself twice to make it clear to the reader that the revelations he spoke of really happened, and he saw it firsthand when he used the phrases, "whether in the body, I cannot tell; or whether out of the body, I cannot tell: God knoweth."

Now let's momentarily accept that the man Paul knew ascended into the third heaven or paradise. Paul would still be here on Planet Earth. How is it that Paul would know that the man he knew "heard unspeakable words, which it is not lawful for a man to utter," unless he ascended along with him and heard it himself or the man descended from the third heaven or paradise and told Paul. Either way you look at it, Paul appears delusional because what he is saying is highly implausible and does not make any sense.

What makes thing far worse for Paul's mental stability was the fact that he believed that his revelations, which he deemed came from God, held some sort of value that Satan (God's rival) saw them as a threat and gave him a thorn in his flesh, in other words, infirmities or a weakness in his flesh, to torture him because of the revelations he could reveal. For this reason, Paul said he begged God three times to take away his thorn in the flesh, and God said to him **"My grace is sufficient for you: for my strength is made perfect in weakness."** In a word, God said NO, and refused to take away Paul's thorn in the flesh, which Satan gave to him. Now ask yourself: Why would God, the creator of heaven and earth with the ability to heal all, refuse to heal Paul? What is strange was Paul's reaction to being told no by God. There was no expressed sadness or disappointment for what Paul deemed tortured him. Rather it's the opposite, saying, in 2 Corinthians 12:9 "Most gladly therefore will I rather glory in my infirmities, that the power of Christ may rest upon me," as though, he never wanted help or to be healed. Even a child could express an emotion of sadness after being told no for the most simplest of things. Again what Paul is saying makes absolutely no sense, especially when you consider who Jesus was and why he came.

John 10:30
I and my Father are one…

John 10:37
If I do not the works of my Father, believe me not. But if I do, though you believe not me, believe the works: that you may know, and believe, that the Father is in me, and I in him.

Jesus and God (the Father) was one in the same. When Jesus performed all his miracles, cured all manner of sickness and disease, and healed the lunatics and those possessed with devils, you can say it was God. So again, why would God refuse to heal Paul, a servant and a minister of Jesus Christ of his infirmities that tormented him?

According to the scriptures, it would appear the reason why Jesus came (his purpose on the earth) was for the lost sheep of the house of Israel, the Jews (God's chosen people).

Matthews 15:24
…I am not sent but to the lost sheep of the house of Israel.

Jesus came to convert Jews to the new way, meaning the Jews had to repent and be baptized in the name of Jesus. Then they could receive forgiveness for their sin(s). This was the gospel (the good news) that Jesus came preaching only to the Jews and healing them of all their infirmities. This matters because of who Paul claimed to be. It is recorded in the book of Acts (21:39 and 22:3) that Paul was a Jew. Then Jesus, who is one with God, also came to heal Paul of his infirmities.

Therefore, it makes no sense that God would say to Paul, a minister of Jesus Christ who sought His help, **"My grace is sufficient for you: for my strength is made perfect in weakness,"** and not take away the thorn in his flesh. This would be the equivalence of God and Jesus saying to Paul, "I want you to suffer physically in your flesh by the hand of Satan and, at the same time, preach to the masses Our message of salvation." What Paul seemed to be saying, makes God an ally with Satan against him. In other words, Paul was making himself, the new Job (from the book of Job) whom God allowed Satan to torture financially, emotionally, mentally and physically.

Job 1:8
   The LORD said to Satan, Have you considered my servant Job...

Now the question is: Could Paul's sin of coveting be related to his thorn in the flesh? Yes. When you look at the actual order of the New Testament books in most Bibles, especially the King James Version, Romans comes before 2 Corinthians. When you place the New Testament books in chronological order as they were written, then 2 Corinthians was written before Romans. (See Appendix 1: New Testament Books (Current/Chronological Order)) When you analyze Paul's writings in 2 Corinthians together with Romans (chapter 7), a creative story emerges between the two of them that just might clear things up a bit.

Paul's explanation of God not taking away or healing his "thorn in the flesh" ties directly with his addiction of coveting. In 2 Corinthians, Paul was laying the groundwork to blame God for his sinful nature by saying God chose not to heal the thorn in his flesh and as a result "sin," the messenger of Satan continued to exist in him. This same sin produced in him all manner of covetous desire, in other words, his addiction.

Therefore, in Paul's mind, there was no reason for him to take responsibility for his own actions or stop his evil ways because, according to Paul, it was never him. It was "sin," the messenger of Satan, still living in him because God did not take away the thorn in Paul's flesh after he begged God, his Creator three times to do so.

Paul's letters to the churches at Corinth and Rome was his way of trying to justify his own actions, which he deemed evil, by blaming sin and God. Coveting (men, women, children, or animals) was Paul's addiction. He told you as much when he stated he was of the tribe of Benjamin.

Romans 11:1
    … I am an Israelite, of the seed of Abraham, of the tribe of Benjamin.

The same tribe, that surrounded the Old Man's house (in the book of Judges 19), and wanted to rape the Levite inside. The same tribe, that took the Concubine and *"abused her all the night until the morning."*

The same tribe, that went to war against the other eleven tribes and was nearly wipe out, because they would not see justice done for the Concubine, who was gang raped to death. The same tribe, that never took responsibility for coveting her (the Concubine) and the same tribe which never repented. So, why would Paul? It is who he was.

Romans 7:7–25

I had not known sin, but by the law: for I had not known lust, except the law had said: You shall not covet. But sin, taking occasion by the commandment, worked in me all manner of concupiscence. For without the law sin was dead. For I was alive without the law once: but when the commandment came, sin revived, and I died. And the commandment, which was ordained to life, I found to be to death. For sin, taking occasion by the commandment, deceived me, and by it slew me. Wherefore the law is holy, and the commandment holy, and just, and good. Was then that which is good made death to me? God forbid. But sin, that it might appear sin, working death in me by that which is good; that sin by the commandment might become exceeding sinful. For we know that the law is spiritual: but I am carnal, sold under sin. For that which I do, I allow not: for what I would, that do I not; but what I hate, that do I. If then I do that which I would not, I consent to the law that it is good. Now then it is no more I that do it, but sin that dwelleth in me. For I know that in me (that is, in my flesh,) dwelleth no good thing: for to will is present with me; but how to perform that which is good, I find not. For the good that I would, I do not: but the evil which I would not, that I do. Now if I do that I would not, it is no more I that do it, but sin that dwelleth in me. I find then a law, that, when I would do good, evil is present with me. For I delight in the law of God after the inward man: But I see another law in my members, warring against the law of my mind, and bringing me into captivity to the law of sin which is in my members. O wretched man that I am! who shall deliver me from the body of this death? I thank God through

Jesus Christ our Lord. So then with the mind I myself serve the law of God; but with the flesh the law of sin.

Paul's Perspective on The Law

Paul's perspective on the law was to destroy it, because of his sin, which he defined as lust and tied directly to the commandment, You Shall Not Covet.

Romans 7:7
> …I had not known sin, but by the law: for I had not known lust, except the law had said: You shall not covet.

The law Paul spoke of in Romans 7:7, in actuality, was the commandment, You Shall Not Covet. To be clear, the law does not say, You Shall Not Covet. The commandments and the laws were mentioned as two separate things. They are not interchangeable; nor are they the same. For example:

Genesis 26:5
> … Abraham obeyed my voice, and kept my charge, my commandments, my statutes, and my laws.

Exodus 16:28
> And the LORD said to Moses, How long do you refuse: to keep my commandments and my laws?

In Romans 8 through 11, it is clear that Paul's problem was not with the law, but the commandment.

Romans 7:8-11
> Sin, taking occasion by the commandment, worked in me all manner of concupiscence. For without the law sin was dead. For

I was alive without the law once: but when the commandment came, sin revived, and I died. And the commandment, which was ordained to life, I found to be to death. For sin, taking occasion by the commandment, deceived me, and by it slew me.

Now the question is: Why was Paul trying to make the commandment, You Shall Not Covet, a part of the law? The only plausible reason for Paul to want this commandment to be seen as a part of the law is this; He was a Jew.

Acts 22:3
Paul said, I am a Jew of Tarsus, a city in Cilicia...

Therefore, no matter what happened to the Old Testament law, the commandment, You Shall Not Covet, which came directly from God to the children of Israel, would still be in effect for Paul. There is no ambiguity concerning the commandments. In the gospel of Matthew, chapters 19, Jesus spoke plainly concerning all the commandments.

Matthews 19:17
There is none good but one, that is, God: but if you will enter into life, keep the commandments.

Paul needed a way to destroy the commandment, You Shall Not Covet, which he deemed deceived him and brought him death. So, the law was a good bet. Now the question is: How would Paul destroy the law?

It is commonly taught throughout the Christian community that Jesus' death on the cross as the sacrificial Lamb was to satisfy or fulfill the Old Testament law. This teaching is based on Jesus saying in the gospel of Matthew what he came to do with the law.

Matthews 5:17-18

Think not that I come to destroy the law, or the prophets: I did not come to destroy, but to fulfil. I say to you, until heaven and earth pass, not one jot or tittle shall pass from the law, till all is fulfilled.

The scriptures are not specific as to how Jesus was to satisfy or fulfill the law. Although, it is clear in the gospel of Matthew, Jesus said he did <u>not</u> come to destroy the law. In fact, Jesus said in the gospel of Luke, he came to fulfill the law of the things which concerned him. This alone does not make sense because the law says nothing concerning Jesus Christ.

Luke 24:44

Jesus said to them, **these are the words which I spoke to you, while I was yet with you, that all things must be fulfilled, which were written in the law of Moses, and in the prophets, and in the psalms, concerning me.**

Regardless, of which passage you believe or think might be true, it is commonly accepted in the Christian community that the law died with Jesus on the cross and those who believe in Jesus Christ are now under grace. However, theologians, along with church leaders, all cite Paul's own letter to the Colossians for that acceptance.

Colossians 2:13–14

> You, being dead in your sins and the uncircumcision of your flesh, has Jesus quickened together with him, having forgiven you all trespasses; blotting out the handwriting of ordinances (the Law) that was against us, which was contrary to us, and took it out of the way, nailing it to his cross.

It is well documented that Paul had long dismissed the Old Testament law as being relevant in his life, with his own writings. Paul seemed successful in convincing Christians and others that the Old Testament law is no longer needed for the forgiveness of sin, because Jesus Christ, the sacrificial Lamb of God had cleansed the sins of the world for all who believe in him.

Galatians 2:19–21

> For I through the law am dead to the law, that I might live to God. I am crucified with Christ: nevertheless I live; yet not I, but Christ liveth in me: and the life which I now live in the flesh I live by the faith of the Son of God, who loved me, and gave himself for me. I do not frustrate the grace of God: for if righteousness come by the law, then Christ is dead in vain.

Romans 6:14

> For sin sh+all not have dominion over you: for you are not under the law, but under grace.

However, Paul's problem was still the commandment, You Shall Not Covet, which is defined and not dependent on any law. The commandment clearly states what you should not do.

Exodus 20:17

You shall not covet thy neighbor's house. You shall not covet thy neighbor's wife, nor his manservant, nor his maidservant, nor his ox, nor his ass, nor any thing that is thy neighbor's.

Therefore, Paul needed to make one commandment a part of the law. Then he could tie all commandments to the law, which would include, You Shall Not Covet. If Paul was to try to tie the commandment, You Shall Not Covet to the law, he would have had a far difficult time doing so, because the law says nothing directly concerning the commandment itself. That is why Paul chose adultery, in his attempt to make the commandment a part of the law. The commandment simply says, You Shall Not Commit Adultery, whereas the law in Leviticus concerning adultery says the following:

Leviticus 20:10

The man that commit adultery with another man's wife, even he that commit adultery with his neighbor's wife, the adulterer and the adulteress shall surely be put to death.

The word adultery is not defined in the commandment or the law. Strictly looking at the law, you must be willing to accept that the word "adultery," means a sexual interaction. This will make it easier to analyze the scriptures. In Romans 7:1–3, Paul put forth his attempt to make the commandment, You Shall Not Commit Adultery a part of the law, based on the lie that a woman is tied to her husband all the days of his life.

Romans 7:1–3

> Know not, brethren…that the law has dominion over a man
> as long as he lives? For the woman which has a husband is
> bound by the law to her husband so long as he lives; but if the
> husband be dead, she is loosed from the law of her husband.
> So then if, while her husband lives, she be married to another
> man, she shall be called an adulteress: but if her husband be
> dead, she is free from that law; so that she is no adulteress,
> although she is married to another man.

To be clear, what Paul was saying is this, when a man and a woman
marry, they are bound to the law to stay married, as long as the
husband lives. If the husband dies, she is free under the law to marry
someone else. However, if her husband was still alive and she married another man, she would be called an adulteress (meaning she
had broken the commandment, You Shall Not Commit Adultery).
If her first husband died while she was still married to another man,
then, the law would set her free from the commandment, You Shall
Not Commit Adultery and she would no longer be an adulteress.

There are several problems with Paul's assertion to make the commandment, You Shall Not Commit Adultery, a part of the law.

1. Adultery is based on a sexual interaction.
2. Marriage is an agreement, which may or may not involve sex.
3. The Old Testament law does not define marriage.

In addition, there is no law that says a woman is bound to her husband as long as he lives. In fact, the law says just the opposite.

Deuteronomy 24:1–4

> When a man has taken a wife and it came to pass that she has no favor in his eyes, because he has found some uncleanness in her. Then let him write her a bill of divorcement, and put it in her hand, and send her out of his house. When she is out of his house, she may go and be another man's wife. If the latter husband hate her, and write her a bill of divorcement, and put it in her hand, and send her out of his house; or if the latter husband died, which took her to be his wife. Her former husband, who sent her away cannot take her back again as his wife, after that she is defiled.

According to Old Testament law, a woman is free from her husband with a bill of divorcement (a piece a paper), while her husband is still alive. When she marries another man, she is not called an adulteress nor becomes an adulteress. If a woman leaves her husband (without a bill of divorcement), she would still be married to him, although they were apart. Therefore, any sexual interaction between her and any other man (not her husband) would fall under God's commandment, You Shall Not Commit Adultery and the law, Leviticus 20:10. Then, according to the law, she is an adulteress and could be put to death along with the man who committed adultery with her. Notwithstanding, there were two or three witnesses to the act of adultery for anyone to be punished. If, Leviticus 20:10 no longer existed, it would have no affect on the commandment, You Shall Not Commit Adultery. Therefore, Paul's attempt failed to show that the commandment, You Shall Not Commit Adultery, was a part of the law, or dependent on the law.

Nevertheless, Paul later wrote his letter to the Ephesians and declared to the saints and the faithful that all the commandments were "abolished" through the cross, which was more than likely based on his false assertion of the commandment, You Shall Not Commit Adultery, being a part of the law.

Ephesians 2:13–16

Now in Christ Jesus you who sometimes were far off are made near by the blood of Christ. For he is our peace, who has made both one, and has broken down the middle wall of partition between us; **Having abolished in his flesh the enmity, even the law of commandments contained in ordinances (the Law)**, to make in himself one new man, therefore making peace, that Jesus might reconcile both to God in one body by the cross, having slain the enmity thereby.

If, Paul believed that the commandments were really abolished, then why would he then resurrect the commandment, Honor your father and mother, four chapters later?

Ephesians 6:1

Children, obey your parents in the Lord: for this is right. Honor thy father and mother; which is the first commandment with promise; that it may be well with you, and you may live long on the earth.

Paul was not always against God's commandments. When he wrote his first letter to the Corinthians, concerning circumcision, Paul stated that keeping the commandments was most important.

1 Corinthians 7:19

> Circumcision is nothing, and uncircumcision is nothing, but the keeping of the commandments of God.

Paul being for the commandments then, now, makes it clear that the commandment, You Shall Not Covet, actually caught him by surprise.

Romans 7:9–10

> For I was alive without the law once: but when the commandment came, sin revived, and I died, and the commandment, which was ordained to life, I found to be to death.

This goes to show that Paul was not against all the commandments, only the one that personally affected him. Remember, Paul said, "by the law is the knowledge of sin" (Romans 3:20). Then abolishing the law along with the commandment, You Shall Not Covet, was for his own purpose; so, he would not have to acknowledge his own evil actions as sin.

Romans 4:15

> Because the law work wrath: where there is no law, there is no transgression (sin).

Now let's just say the law was bad and outdated with its animal and blood sacrifices and no longer needed. Let's also say that Paul's reasoning for wanting the law destroyed was warranted because Jesus redeemed all under the law to grace. Ask yourself: What is wrong with any of these commandments that they should be added to law and abolished?

- Honor Your Mother and Father
- You Shall Not Commit Adultery
- You Shall Not Murder
- You Shall Not Steal
- You Shall Not Bear False Witness (Lie)
- You Shall Not Covet

Paul believed he was successful at linking a commandment to the law, the law to Jesus Christ, and Jesus Christ to the cross. That is why, Paul made up out of thin air;

- The "law of God," which encompassed God's laws and commandments.
- The "law of sin," which represented his sinful nature, that is, the thorn in his flesh (his addiction to coveting men, women, children, or animals).
- The "law of the Spirit of Life," which represented freedom, making all thing new again.

Now Paul gets the outcome that he chose for himself, redemption.

Romans 7:22–25

For I delight in the law of God after the inward man: I see another law in my members, warring against the law of my mind, and bringing me into captivity to the law of sin which is in my members. O wretched man that I am! who shall deliver me from the body of this death? I thank God through Jesus Christ our Lord. So then with the mind I myself serve the law of God; but with the flesh the law of sin.

Romans 8:1–2

> There is now no condemnation to them which are in Christ
> Jesus, who walk not after the flesh, but after the Spirit. For
> the law of the Spirit of life in Christ Jesus has made me free
> from the law of sin and death.

Finally, there would be total absolution for any and all of Paul's
actions, and in his mind, he was free from the commandment, You
Shall Not Covet. In fact, Paul was free from all the commandments,
including You Shall Not Kill and You Shall Not Steal, leaving him
free to serve two masters sin and God.

It's all About Paul

Paul's overall perspective on his sin and the law was self-serving. His uncontrolled illicit sexual appetite (lust) appears to be the reason for all his lies. Paul lied repeatedly and often to achieve the goal or the outcome that he wanted for himself, to be free from the commandment, You Shall Not Covet. Remember, Paul said sin produced in him all manner of covetous desire. Therefore, his letter to the Romans was not written for you or the Church (as you may believe them to be), but for himself, to justify his addiction to coveting, and at the same time to represent himself as a servant and a minister of Jesus Christ speaking for God, and against men and women who have consensual same-sex relations.

Romans 1:26–27

God gave them up to vile affections: for even their women did change the natural use into that which is against nature: likewise also the men, leaving the natural use of the woman, burned in their lust one toward another; men with men working that which is unseemly, and receiving in themselves that recompense of their error which was meet.

Paul projected his deviant sexual behavior onto men and women in a consensual same-sex relationship because he was the one with the deviant sexual behavioral problems. In Romans 1:27, Paul said, "the men, leaving the natural use of the woman, burned in their lust one toward another." These men Paul was speaking of were choosing to be together, like any other couple in a good and healthy relationship. This was not the case with Paul his deviant sexual behavioral problems were evil, unhealthy, and not about choice.

Romans 1:28-32

> Even as they did not like to retain God in their knowledge, God gave them over to a reprobate mind, to do those things which are not convenient; Being filled with all unrighteousness, <u>fornication</u>, wickedness, <u>covetousness</u>, maliciousness; full of envy, <u>murder</u>, debate, deceit, malignity; whisperers, Backbiters, haters of God, despiteful, proud, boasters, inventors of evil things, <u>disobedient to parents</u>, Without understanding, covenantbreakers, without natural affection, implacable, unmerciful: Who knowing the judgment of God, that they which commit such things are worthy of death, not only do the same, but have pleasure in them that do them.

It's as though, Paul was saying that men and women who have consensual same-sex relations are predisposed to unrighteous and wicked acts. What stands out more than anything in Romans 1:28, was Paul saying, "They did not like to retain God in their knowledge." Ask yourself: How would Paul know that "they did not like to retain God in their knowledge?" Did he ask God? Maybe God spoke to Paul in a dream, saying, "Hey, Paul, men and women who have consensual same-sex relations don't keep me on their minds, so I, God, will give them over to a depraved mind to be unrighteous, to fornicate, be wicked, to be covetous, malicious, full of envy, murder, debate, deceit, malignity, whisperer, backbiter, hater of God, despiteful, proud, boaster, inventor of evil things, disobedient to parents, without understanding, covenant breaker, without natural affection, implacable and unmerciful." It doesn't make any sense, unless there was an inner personal struggle between Paul and God. Remember, in Romans 7:14, Paul said he was "carnal" and "sold under sin." Therefore, if what Paul said was true, which no one should doubt, then, it was Paul who did not always retain God on his mind.

When you analyze Romans 1:29–32, a picture starts to develop about Paul that should make sense. You can surmise from the book of Acts and Paul's own writings that he was more than likely talking about himself and again projecting his own dark and what he deemed were evil actions onto men and women who have consensual same-sex relations. Everything Paul wrote seemed to be very specific and of a personal nature. For example, Paul included three of God commandments, You Shall Not Covet (covetousness), You Shall Not Kill (murder) and Honor your Father and Mother (disobedient to parents). The same God that gave those commandments also said, You Shall Not Commit Adultery, You Shall Not Steal and You Shall Not Bear False Witness (Lie). So, why were they not included? When you analyze what Paul wrote (in verses 29–31), word for word, it appears to be a self-analysis of his own life, which could all be summed up in his own words.

Romans 7:18 -19

> For I know that in me (that is, in my flesh,) dwelleth no good thing: for the will is present with me; but how to perform that which is good, I find not. For the good that I would, I do not: but the evil which I would not, that I do.

However, when you take a closer look at the four major things Paul listed, <u>coveteousness</u> (already noted), <u>fornication</u>, <u>murder</u>, and a <u>hater of God</u> all identify with who Paul was.

Fornication

There is no mention of Paul ever having a wife or a concubine in the scriptures. Looking strictly at the scriptures as they are written, Paul represented himself as a single man in his first letter to the Corinthians.

1 Corinthians 7:7-9

For I would that all men were even as I myself. But every man has his proper gift of God, one after this manner, and another after that. I say therefore to the unmarried and widows, it is good for them if they abide even as I, but if they cannot contain themselves, let them marry: for it is better to marry than to burn. ..

In Paul's first letter to Timothy, he specifically used the phrase, "my own son."

1 Timothy 1:2

To Timothy, my own son in the faith: Grace, mercy, and peace, from God our Father and Jesus Christ our Lord.

In Paul's second letter to Timothy, he used the phrase, "my dearly beloved son."

2 Timothy 1:1-6

Paul, an apostle of Jesus Christ by the will of God, according to the promise of life which is in Christ Jesus, to Timothy, my dearly beloved son... Greatly desiring to see you, being mindful of your tears, that I may be filled with joy; when I call to remembrance the unfeigned faith that is in you, which was in your grandmother Lois and your mother Eunice, which I am persuaded is in you....

2 Timothy 3:14-15

But continue in the things which you have learned and have been assured of, knowing of whom you have learned them, from a child you have known the holy scriptures, which are able to make you wise to salvation through faith which is in Christ Jesus.

In Paul's letter to Philemon, he used the phrase, "my son."

Philemon 1:10-21

I implore you for my son Onesimus, whom I have begotten in my bonds: in time past was to you unprofitable, but now profitable to you and to me... receive him, my own bowels (son).

Therefore, taking the scriptures listed into account, Paul could have been a fornicator and worthy of death.

Murder

Paul said in Romans 1:32, "they which commit such things are worthy of death, not only do the same, but have pleasure in them that do them." In the book of Acts, Paul (formerly known as Saul) consented in the stoning of Stephen, a man of God who was killed.

Acts 7:58–8:1

> They cast him (Stephen) out of the city and stoned him. The witnesses laid down their clothes at a young man's feet, whose name was Saul, and they stoned Stephen, while he was calling upon God, and saying, Lord Jesus, receive my spirit.… and Saul was consenting to his death.

Therefore, based on Paul consenting to the death of a man of God, he would have been worthy of death.

Hater of God

☙ It is written,

In the book of Acts, Paul (formerly known as Saul) persecuted the Church. Paul confirmed this, in his first letter to the Corinthians.

Acts 8:3

> As for Saul, he made havock of the church, entering into every house, and committed them to prison.

1 Corinthians 15:9

> I am the least of the apostles, not fit to be called an apostle, because I persecuted the church of God.

☙ It is written,

God said: Keep my commandments.

Exodus 20:5-6

I the LORD am a jealous God, visiting the iniquity of the fathers upon the children to the third and fourth generation of them that hate me, and showing mercy to thousands of them that love me, and keep my commandments.

Jesus said: **Keep the commandments.**

Matthews 19:17

There is none good but one, that is, God: but if you will enter into life, keep the commandments.

Paul rejected Gods laws and commandments and in his mind set out to destroy them all, because one of God's commandments, You Shall Not Covet, offended him. This alone makes Paul, full of wickedness, maliciousness; full of envy, debate, deceit, malignity; whisperer, backbiter, despiteful, proud, boaster, inventor of evil things, without understanding, covenant breaker, without natural affection, implacable and unmerciful. Therefore, Paul was anti-God and worthy of death.

Some may conclude that God gave up on men and women who have consensual same-sex relations and believe they are unclean, and the affection they share is vile, because of what they were taught or somehow share that same view. Although no one should believe or conclude that God, the creator of heaven and earth, gave men and women who have same-sex relations over to a reprobate mind "to do" other immoral things. If this is the case, then they should accept that fornication, which is consenting sex among single men and women, is one of those unrighteous and wicked acts. Then those who commit fornication are themselves predisposed to other unrighteous and wicked acts, such as covetousness, maliciousness; being full of envy, murder, debate, deceitful, malignity; whisperer, backbiter, haters of God, despiteful, proud, boaster, inventor of evil things, disobedient to parents, without understanding, covenant breaker, without natural affection, implacable and unmerciful.

According to Paul, there is no difference between rape, murder, and consenting sex among single men and women. As a result, if anyone commit(s) or have pleasure in someone else who commit(s) any of these acts (listed in Romans 1:29–31), he or she is worthy of death.

Now it should be clear, that it was Paul who had the problem:

- with God's authority
  - His laws
  - His commandments
- with Satan
- with coveting (lust)
  - men
  - women
  - children
  - or animal(s)
- with telling lies
- with staying focused on God
- with consensual-sex
  - fornication
  - adultery
  - same-sex relations (to be specific)

* with mental illness
* with wanting to be God

Therefore, to be absolutely clear, it was all about Paul.

CHAPTER 10

THE THORN IN THE FLESH

THE MAIN REASON FOR THIS chapter is to show that Paul's mental stability is a factor, because he is the predominant writer of the New Testament. (See Appendix II: New Testament Books (By Author)) Also, to demonstrate two things: How others saw Paul's thorn in the flesh, and how far reference materials, such as the *Holman Bible Dictionary* and the *Wycliffe Bible Encyclopedia*, would go to explain Paul's own writings.

When you search both reference books for additional information or an explanation about Paul's thorn in the flesh, they both conclude the same thing, that Paul's thorn in the flesh was not an illness, but an enemy.

PAUL'S THORN IN THE FLESH

2 Corinthians 12:1–9

> It is not expedient for me to glory. I will come to visions and revelations of the Lord. I knew a man in Christ more than fourteen years ago, (whether in the body, I cannot

tell; or whether out of the body, I cannot tell: God knows). He was caught up to the third heaven and I knew such a man (whether in the body, or out of the body, I cannot tell: God knows). He was caught up into paradise and heard unspeakable words, which it is not lawful for a man to utter. In this man I will glory. Yet in myself I will not glory, except in my infirmities. Although, I would desire to glory, I shall not be a fool, for I will say the truth, but for now I will hold my tongue, lest any man should think of me above that which he see me to be, or that he hear of me. **(7)**Lest I should be exalted above measure through the abundance of revelations, there was given to me a thorn in the flesh, the messenger of Satan to buffet me, lest I should be exalted above measure. **(8)**For this thing I sought the Lord three times, that it might depart from me. **(9)**And he said to me: **My grace is sufficient for you: for my strength is made perfect in weakness.** Most gladly will I glory in my infirmities that the power of Christ may rest upon me.

THE HOLMAN BIBLE DICTIONARY

The *Holman Bible Dictionary* provides insight as to what others may have believed Paul's thorn in the flesh to have been. They mentioned three possible illnesses: epilepsy, malaria, and eye disease.

1. Epilepsy is a brain disorder that causes recurring seizures. Symptoms consist of temporary confusion and loss of consciousness.

2. Malaria is a mosquito-borne disease in which the main symptoms are chills, fever, coma, convulsions, and headaches, just to name a few.
3. Eye disease causes visual problems and blindness.

The suggestion of epilepsy gives rise to the fact that others saw Paul's "revelations" (which was the reason he gave for his thorn in the flesh), as some sort of brain disorder. The same with malaria, it gives the impression that Paul could have been in and out consciousness, where his revelations were formed. The eye disease seems to be more of a statement, which says that Paul did not see what he believed he saw, because what he says he saw is far from reality.

The *Holman Bible Dictionary* offered a two-solution strategy to conclude that Paul's "thorn in the flesh" was an enemy.

The first solution:

 ⚘ "A more acceptable solution, however, relates to the context of 2 Corinthians 12:1-10 where "thorn in the flesh" parallels both "messenger of Satan" in verse 7 and the "weaknesses," "insults," "distresses," "persecutions," and "difficulties" of verse 10."

The second solution:

 ⚘ "The Old Testament use of the term thorn also offers some help. In Numbers 33:55; Ezekiel 28:24 we read of enemies who are "thorns" in Israel's side, a constant harrassment to

Israel as the agent of the Lord's redemptive judgments (compare Josh. 23:13; Hos. 2:6)."

The first solution equated Paul's thorn in the flesh (verse 7) with weaknesses, insults, distresses, persecutions, and difficulties (verse 10), using the New International Version Bible. One could conclude that Paul was referring to an enemy, the "messenger of Satan," in verse 10, especially with the use of the word "insults," using the New International Version Bible. The problem is: Paul's "thorn in the flesh" story was concluded in verse 9, not verse 10.

2 Corinthians 12:9

He said to me: **"My grace is sufficient for you: for my strength is made perfect in weakness."** Most gladly therefore will I rather glory in my infirmities, that the power of Christ may rest upon me.

Who delights in weaknesses, insults, hardships, persecution, and difficulties period, especially when dealing with an enemy? The *Holman Bible Dictionary* wants Christians and non-Christians to believe or accept that Paul's thorn in the flesh was an enemy, and using verse 10, out of context appears to help make that point.

The second solution suggested that the word "thorn" could be an enemy based on the Old Testament meaning of the term "thorns," which would mean more than one person or enemies. To support their enemy theory, they cited Numbers 33:55, Joshua 23:13, Ezekiel 28:24, and Hosea 2:6, which are all irrelevant but contain the word "thorn" or "thorns."

* Numbers 33:55

  But if you will not drive out the inhabitants of the land from before you; then it shall come to pass, that those which you let remain of them shall be pricks in your eyes, and <u>thorns</u> in your sides, and shall vex you in the land wherein you dwell.

* Joshua 23:13

  Know for a certainty that the LORD your God will no more drive out any of these nations from before you; but they shall be snares and traps to you, and scourges in your sides, and <u>thorns</u> in your eyes, until you perish from off this good land which the LORD your God has given you.

* Ezekiel 28:24

  There shall be no more a pricking brier to the house of Israel, nor any grieving <u>thorn</u> of all that are round about them, that despised them; and they shall know that I am the Lord GOD.

* Hosea 2:6

  Therefore, behold, I will hedge up your way with <u>thorns</u>, and make a wall, that she shall not find her paths.

It is ironic that the *Holman Bible Dictionary* would choose Ezekiel 28:24, where God stood up for Israel, but not for Paul who claimed to be an Israelite of the tribe of Benjamin, and a minister of Jesus Christ (the Son of God).

Since the *Holman Bible Dictionary* was quoting from the New International Version Bible, then they should have quoted that Paul used the phrase "a thorn in my flesh." Therefore, it makes no sense for Paul's thorn in the flesh to have been a person or a physical enemy with the phrase, "a thorn <u>in my flesh</u>."

THE WYCLIFFE BIBLE ENCYCLOPEDIA

An overall view of the *Wycliffe Bible Encyclopedia* on the topic of Paul's thorn in the flesh, it is more than likely they are citing scriptures from the King James Version of the Bible.

The *Wycliffe Bible Encyclopedia* suggested four scenarios for Paul's thorn in the flesh, which they provided an explanation for only the first two.

1. "persistent carnal desires or fleshly temptation"
2. "feelings of guilt stemming from his having formerly persecuted the church"
3. "some form of physical or nervous ailment"
4. "a personal enemy who sought to slander and discredit him"
    * "Regarding the first, he found victory through the indwelling Spirit of God (Rom 8:5-13). Regarding the second he knew that the grace of Jesus Christ had fully absolved him of his past crime (1 Tim 1:13-16). Whatever was the nature of his thorn, it did not prevent his continuing in an extremely active ministry which included long journeys on foot."

The first and third items listed prior seemed to be spot-on, whereas the second and fourth scenarios listed, are a farce in determining what Paul's thorn in the flesh really was. However, when you analyze the fourth item listed, it opens the door to a better understanding as to why Paul wrote both Corinthian letters.

1 and 3

The first item, suggest that Paul's "thorn in the flesh" was his persistent carnal desires. However, the *Wycliffe Bible Encyclopedia* dismissed this idea, stating that Paul "found victory through the indwelling Spirit of God" and by citing Paul's own letter to the Romans 8:5–13.

Romans 8:5–13

> For those that are after the flesh, do mind the things of the flesh; but those that are after the Spirit the things of the Spirit. For to be carnally minded is death; but to be spiritually minded is life and peace. Because the carnal mind is enmity against God: for it is not subject to the law of God, neither indeed can be. So then they that are in the flesh cannot please God. But you are not in the flesh, but in the Spirit, if the Spirit of God dwells in you. If any man does not have the Spirit of Christ, he is none of his. If Christ be in you, the body is dead because of sin; but the Spirit is life because of righteousness. But if the Spirit of him that raised up Jesus from the dead dwell in you, he that raised up Christ from the dead shall also quicken your mortal bodies by his Spirit that dwelleth in you. Therefore, brethren, we are debtors, not to the flesh, to live after the flesh. For if you live after the flesh, you shall die: but if you through the Spirit do mortify the deeds of the body, you shall live.

It would appear that the *Wycliffe Bible Encyclopedia* unintentionally defined Paul's problem when they stated that Paul "found victory through the indwelling Spirit of God," which is a conclusion. Therefore, Paul's thorn in the flesh must have been his persistent carnal desire, in other words, his addiction to coveting. Then they should have also noted:

Romans 8:1-2

There is now no condemnation to them which are in Christ Jesus... For the law of the Spirit of life in Christ Jesus has made me free from the law of sin and death.

———◆———

The third item suggest that others have formed an opinion that Paul suffered from some sort of physical ailment. The *Wycliffe Bible Encyclopedia* listed a total of six possible diseases to explain his visions and revelations for which he received his thorn in the flesh.

1. "Epilepsy"
2. "Acute Ophthalmic or eye trouble"
3. "Malarial Fever"
4. "Hysteria or Melancholy"
5. "Sick Headache"
6. "Nervous Exhaustion"

Some of the sicknesses and diseases listed demonstrate that Paul more than likely had a brain injury or an illness that caused him to hallucinate. The fact that the *Wycliffe Bible Encyclopedia* included "hysteria," suggest that Paul could have suffered from a traumatic injury which caused him to become mentally unstable.

2 and 4

The second item listed, suggest that Paul had "feelings of guilt because he once persecuted the church." It makes absolutely no sense to suggest that Satan gave Paul a thorn in the flesh because he persecuted the church. One would think Satan would have rewarded Paul for his actions against the church. The *Wycliffe Bible Encyclopedia* ruled it out, stating that Paul "knew that the grace of Jesus Christ had fully absolved him of his past crimes" again by citing Paul's own writings for his absolution.

1 Timothy 1:13-15

> Who was before a blasphemer, and a persecutor, and injurious: but I obtained mercy, because I did it ignorantly in unbelief. The grace of our Lord was exceeding abundant... This is a faithful saying, and worthy of all acceptation, that Christ Jesus came into the world to save sinners; of whom I am chief.

The fourth and final item listed, suggest that Paul's thorn in the flesh was a "personal enemy who sought to slander and discredit him." To support their theory, the *Wycliffe Bible Encyclopedia* put forth two explanations.

- "In the Old Testament a 'thorn' was a rather common idiom for a human enemy... (Numbers 33:55; Joshua 23:13). Ezekiel refs to the enemies of Israel as 'a pricking brier' and 'any grieving thorn.'"

- * "A study of the phrase 'thorn in the flesh' and of its context in Paul's defense of his apostleship (2 Cor. 10–13) indicates that it probably refers to a person, not an illness."

First

They suggest that Paul's thorn in the flesh was an enemy based on the Old Testament use of the word "thorn," by citing the same verses as the *Holman Bible Dictionary*, which were all irrelevant, but contained the words "thorn" or "thorns."

Second

They suggest that Paul's thorn in the flesh was in defense of his apostleship, which they concluded was a "personal enemy" (one person). In order to prove their theory that Paul's thorn in the flesh was a personal enemy, they cited the following:

2 Corinthians 12:10–13.

(10)Therefore I take pleasure in <u>infirmities</u>, in <u>reproaches</u>, in <u>necessities</u>, in <u>persecutions</u>, in <u>distresses</u> for Christ's sake: for when I am weak, then am I strong. (11)I am a fool in glorying; you have compelled me: for I ought to have been commended of you: for in nothing am I behind the very chiefest apostles, though I be nothing. (12)Truly the signs of an apostle were worked among you in all patience, in signs, and wonders, and mighty deeds. (13)What is it you were inferior to other churches, except that I myself was not burdensome to you? Forgive me this wrong.

None of the verses listed appear to have anything to do with any one person or an enemy. When you analyze all four scriptures, they have absolutely nothing to do with Paul's thorn in the flesh. However, they are very interesting, because they provide insight as to why Paul wrote both first and second Corinthian letters, which was money.

Now again, Paul's "thorn in the flesh" story was concluded in verse 9, not verse 10. Verse 10 is the beginning of Paul's conclusion for his entire letter (2 Corinthians). Looking only at verse 10, it is a conclusion of a whole list of things that Paul wrote about in detail in the prior chapter that happened to him during his ministry (2 Corinthians 11:20–33).

In Reproaches:
2 Corinthians 11:20-21

> For you suffer, if a man bring you into bondage, if a man devour you, if a man take of you, if a man exalt himself, if a man smite you on the face. I speak as concerning reproach...

In Infirmities:
2 Corinthians 11:24-25

> Of the Jews five times received I forty stripes save one. Three times was I beaten with rods, once was I stoned, three times I suffered shipwreck, a night and a day I have been in the deep;

In Distresses:
2 Corinthians 11:26

Journeying often, in perils of waters, in perils of robbers, in perils by my own countrymen, in perils by the heathen, in perils in the city, in perils in the wilderness, in perils in the sea, in perils among false brethren.

In Necessities:
2 Corinthians 11:27

In weariness and painfulness, in watching often, in hunger and thirst, in fasting often, in cold and nakedness…

In Persecutions:
2 Corinthians 11:31-33

The God and Father of our Lord Jesus Christ, which is blessed for evermore, know that I lie not. In Damascus the governor…with a garrison

(stationed troops), desirous to apprehend me, and through a window in a basket was I let down by the wall, and escaped his hands.

When you look only at verse 11, what stands out is the word "you." Some may conclude that Paul was referring to an enemy in opposition to his teachings of God and Christ based solely on the word "you." However, when you look at the entire verse in context, it seems less likely.

2 Corinthians 12:11

…for I ought to have been commended of you: for in nothing am I behind the very chiefest apostles, though I be nothing.

The word "you" does not refer to a single person or an enemy. In fact, the statement "for I ought to have been commended of you" refers to whom Paul was writing his letter, the church of God at Corinth and all the saints.

2 Corinthians 1:1
> Paul, an apostle of Jesus Christ by the will of God, and Timothy our brother, to the church of God which is at Corinth, with all the saints which are in Achaia.

Now when you analyze verses 12 and 13, Paul wanted the church at Corinth to recognize his authority and his apostleship.

2 Corinthians 12:12-13
> Truly the signs of an apostle were worked among you in all patience, in signs, wonders, and mighty deeds. What is it that you were inferior to other churches, except that I myself was not burdensome to you? Forgive me this wrong.

The main reason Paul was writing his second letter to the church at Corinth was because they challenged his authority to speak for Christ in his first letter (1 Corinthians) to them.

2 Corinthians 13:3
> Since you seek proof of Christ speaking in me, to you is not weak, but is mighty in you...

Paul's authority was being challenged because of money. In Paul's first letter to the church at Corinth, he ordered the church to take up a weekly collection of money among the saints for his own purposes.

(Many, if not all, Christian churches today take up collections of money in the form of tithes, offerings, or gifts of love on Sunday, the first day of the week. Some churches take up more than one collection weekly.)

1 Corinthians 16:1-3

Now concerning the collection for the saints, as I have given order to the churches of Galatia, you also do the same. On the first day of the week let every one of you lay in store, as God has prospered him, that there be no gatherings when I come. When I come, whomsoever you shall approve by your letters, them will I send to bring your liberality to Jerusalem.

Paul's second letter to the church at Corinth was in response to him being challenged. This was why Paul began his second letter using a more calm and peaceful tone and laying out an excuse for why he needed money (the gift).

2 Corinthians 1:8–11

For we would not, brethren, have you ignorant of our trouble which came to us in Asia, that we were pressed out of measure, above strength, insomuch that we despaired even of life: But we had the sentence of death in ourselves, that we should not trust in ourselves, but in God which raise the dead. Who delivered us from so great a death, and do deliver, in whom we trust that will yet deliver us. You also helping together by prayer for us, that for the gift bestowed upon us by the means of many persons, thanks may be given by many on our behalf.

Paul wrote in detail throughout 2 Corinthians concerning the gift or bounty (money) he was expecting from the church at Corinth and all the saints. For example:

2 Corinthians 9:5-7

> Therefore I thought it necessary to exhort the brethren, that they would go before you, and make up before hand your bounty, you had notice before, that the same should be ready, as a matter of bounty, and not as of covetousness. But this I say, he that sow sparingly shall reap also sparingly; and he that sow bountifully shall reap also bountifully. Every man according as he purposes in his heart, so let him give; not grudgingly, or of necessity: for God loves a cheerful giver...

II CORINTHIANS 12:10-13
CONCLUSION

Now to sum up 2 Corinthians 12:10–13, Paul was saying that he should have been commended by the church at Corinth and all the saints for everything he suffered (infirmities, reproaches, necessities, persecutions, and distresses) in bringing them the gospel of God at no cost.

2 Corinthians 11:7-9

> Have I committed an offence in abasing myself that you might be exalted, because I have preached to you the gospel of God freely? I robbed other churches, taking wages of them, to do you service. And when I was present with you, and wanted, I was chargeable to no man: for that which was lacking to me

the brethren which came from Macedonia supplied: and in all things I have kept myself from being burdensome to you, and so will I keep myself.

Paul was clearly responding to his authority being challenged because he ordered the church at Corinth to take up a weekly collection of money for his use. Paul's authority to speak for Jesus Christ was the issue being challenged and was more than likely the reason why he changed his title, to appear more authoritarian.

First Corinthians: Paul, called (*to be*) an apostle of Jesus Christ through the will of God and Sosthenes, our brother

Second Corinthians: Paul, an apostle of Jesus Christ by the will of God

First and Second Corinthians were private letters Paul wrote to the church at Corinth to convince them of his authority he believed he had been given by Jesus Christ and God. His letters were never meant for anyone else, and that includes Christians today. It is clear from Paul's first letter to the Corinthians that he was responding to an earlier letter written to him (7:1–2) and expecting a private written response from the church at Corinth (16:1–3).

1 Corinthians 7:1–2

> **Now concerning the things you wrote to me:** It is good for a man not to touch a woman. Nevertheless, to avoid fornication, let every man have his own wife, and let every woman have her own husband.

1 Corinthians 16:1–3

Now concerning the collection for the saints, as I have given order to the churches of Galatia, you also do the same. On the first day of the week let every one of you lay in store, as God has prospered him, that there be no gatherings when I come. And when I come, **whomsoever you shall approve by your letters, them will I send to bring your liberality to Jerusalem.**

All written communications or letters related to First and Second Corinthians have not been revealed. There is no way of knowing whether Paul's first letter to the Corinthians was his first or his tenth. Ask yourself: Why would the church at Corinth seek proof of Jesus Christ speaking through Paul, in 2nd Corinthians 13:3, unless he told them that Jesus Christ was speaking through, by or in him, in one of his letters, which has not yet been revealed? Also, there is no way of knowing whether Paul received the money, gift, or bounty, which the letters were about, because there are no communications or letters to tell us. Therefore, how is Paul's private and incomplete communications or letters with the church at Corinth or any church the Word of God?

Using the scriptures they provided, the *Wycliffe Bible Encyclopedia* concluded that Paul's thorn in the flesh was a "personal enemy who sought to slander and discredit him." Maybe they should have concluded that Paul's thorn in the flesh was his persistent carnal desires, perhaps due to a physical or nervous ailment (mental defect).

1. "persistent carnal desires or fleshly temptation"
2. ~~"feelings of guilt stemming from his having formerly persecuted the church"~~

3. "some form of physical or nervous ailment"

4. ~~"a personal enemy who sought to slander and discredit him"~~

Nonetheless, the *Wycliffe Bible Encyclopedia* closed with Paul's thorn in the flesh, which appears to be written directly to Christians, this way:

* "In his response to his thorn in the flesh Paul demonstrated the proper Christian response to frustration, whatever form it may take. After earnest prayer for its removal, he accepted it and made the best of the situation by the grace of Christ."

Therefore, regardless of what Paul's thorn in the flesh could have been, the proper Christian response is to accept it. Regardless of what *it* is.

CHAPTER 11

Is Paul the New Standard-Bearer?

Jesus said, follow me.

John 10:27-28

> **My sheep hear my voice, and I know them, and they follow me: And I give to them eternal life; and they shall never perish, neither shall any man pluck them out of my hand.**

Paul said, follow him.

1 Corinthians 4:16

> I implore you, be followers of me.

1 Corinthians 11:1-2

> Be followers of me, even as I am of Christ. Now I praise you, brethren, that you remember me in all things, and keep the ordinances, as I delivered them to you.

Many Christians believe and accept Jesus Christ as their standard-bearer. However, Jesus says absolutely nothing about same-sex relationships or marriage. The main thing Jesus remotely teaches concerning sex relates to divorce and adultery.

Matthew 5:32

I say to you, that whosoever shall put away his wife, except for the cause of fornication, causes her to commit adultery: and whosoever shall marry her that is divorced commits adultery.

The reason Jesus gave for a man to divorce his wife is "the cause of fornication," which alone is strange because you would think, if she was his wife, then it would only be adultery and not fornication. Nevertheless, Jesus is talking about adultery, which is sex with someone other than his or her spouse. Now, one would think Jesus spoke about the things that he deemed were important, since he is asking others to follow after him. Therefore, Jesus could have spoken about same-sex relationships or marriage, if it was important to him, but he did not.

Many church leaders under the banner of Christianity are against same-sex relationships and marriage, based solely on the teachings of Paul. Now are Christians supposed to accept what others say about same-sex relationships or marriage, as though Jesus had said it? In other words, when Paul says that God gave "them" up, meaning men and women in a same-sex relationship, is it equal to Jesus Christ saying it himself? If yes, then Christianity is not just about the teachings of Jesus Christ. It has become the teachings of Jesus Christ, Paul, and every pastor, preacher teacher, reverend, bishop, doctor, and priest who believe and teach that God is against same-sex relations. If no, then why is it that the church as a whole care so much about what Paul wrote in Romans 1:26–27? Christians today cannot say it is all about the teachings of Jesus Christ, when they are quoting Paul.

Romans 1:26–32.

> For this cause God gave them up to vile affections: for even their women did change <u>the natural use</u> into that which is against nature: And likewise also the men, leaving <u>the natural use</u> of the woman, burned in their lust one toward another; men with men working that which is unseemly, and receiving in themselves that recompense of their error which was meet. And even as they did not like to retain God in their knowledge, God gave them over to a reprobate mind, to do those things which are not convenient; Being filled with all unrighteousness, fornication, wickedness, covetousness, maliciousness; full of envy, murder, debate, deceit, malignity; whisperers, Backbiters, haters of God, despiteful, proud, boasters, inventors of evil things, disobedient to parents, Without understanding, covenant breakers, without natural affection, implacable, unmerciful: Who knowing the judgment of God, that they which commit such things are worthy of death, not only do the same, but have pleasure in them that do them.

Paul used the words "the natural use," to imply or plant the seed that there is something unnatural about men and women who have same-sex relations. These three words matter most in Paul's letter to the Romans because they have destroyed lives and demonized men and women in or desiring a same-sex relationship or marriage around the world to this very day. When you ask Christians and non-Christians who are against same-sex relations why they oppose it, they tend to use the word "unnatural." Some Christians believe Paul's assertion that God is against men and women who have same-sex relations and believe their affections are unnatural. Others are against same-sex relations because same-sex couples cannot procreate, as they believe God intended, meaning they cannot have children, which happens to be the same reason they are against same-sex marriage.

"Unnatural: 1. Contrary to expected behavior:
contrary to habit, custom, or practice."
Encarta ® World English Dictionary

———

"Unnatural: 2. At variance with the character or
Nature of a person, animal or plant"
Webster's Encyclopedic Unabridged Dictionary

The word "unnatural" is not a bad word from one's own perspective. For men and women who are only attracted to individuals of the opposite sex, it would be unnatural for them to be with someone sexually of the same sex. The same would be true for men and women who are only attracted to individuals of the same sex; it would be unnatural for them to be with someone sexually of the opposite sex. However, for those who justify their stance against same-sex relationships or marriage based on the fact that same-sex couples cannot procreate, they should understand that for many people, having children is a choice. Not every man or woman who come together sexually desire to procreate. There are many men and women who want to have children but can't. Therefore, are men and women in a same-sex relationship or marriage any less natural than a sterile man and his wife or a woman who is unable to conceive with her male companion? The problem with what Paul wrote is this:

he is condemning men and women to death for having consensual sex, and even those who don't, but find pleasure in someone else who does.

Now, one would think that Paul wrote about all the things he deemed were most important to him. A common theme in Paul's letters is that he considered consensual sex, such as: same-sex relations (to be specific), fornication, and adultery to be unrighteous, in other words, a sin. When he mentioned them in his letters, he included despicable things, such as murder, lasciviousness, covetousness, idolatry, and many others to make his point that consensual sex is unrighteous and God is against it. For example,

1 Corinthians 6:9–10

The unrighteous shall not inherit the kingdom of God? Be not deceived: neither <u>fornicators</u>, nor idolaters, nor <u>adulterers</u>, nor effeminate, nor abusers of themselves with mankind, nor thieves, nor covetous, nor drunkards, nor revilers, nor extortioners, shall inherit the kingdom of God.

Galatians 5:19–21

Now the works of the flesh are manifest, which are these; <u>Adultery</u>, <u>fornication</u>, uncleanness, lasciviousness, Idolatry, witchcraft, hatred, variance, emulations, wrath, strife, seditions, heresies, envying, murders, drunkenness, revelling, and such like: I told you before, that they which do such things shall not inherit the kingdom of God.

Ephesians 5:2–6

Be followers of God, as dear children; walk in love, as Christ has loved us, and has given himself for us. But <u>fornication</u>, and all uncleanness, or covetousness, let it not be once named among you, as saints; Neither filthiness, nor foolish talking, nor jesting, which are not convenient: but rather giving of thanks. For this you know, that no whoremonger, nor unclean person, nor covetous man, who is an idolater, has no inheritance in the kingdom of Christ and of God. Let no man deceive you with vain words: because of these things the wrath of God is upon the children of disobedience.

Colossians 3:5–7

Mortify your members which are upon the earth; fornication, uncleanness, inordinate affection, evil concupiscence, and covetousness, which is idolatry:...the wrath of God cometh on the children of disobedience...

Hebrews 13:4

Marriage is honourable in all, and the bed undefiled: but whoremongers and adulterers God will judge.

1 Thessalonians 4:1–3

...We implore you, brethren, and exhort you by the Lord Jesus, that you have received of us how you ought to walk and to please God, so you would abound more and more. For you know what commandments we gave you by the Lord Jesus. This is the will of God, even your sanctification that you should abstain from fornication.

When you analyze Paul's letters to the churches, his stance against consensual same-sex relations among the Romans was the same position he held against consensual sex between men and women among the Colossians, Corinthians, Ephesians, Galatians, Hebrews, and Thessalonians. According to Paul, the only way to abstain from fornication is to marry. Therefore, Paul believed that no one should have sex unless it is done his way through marriage between a man and a woman, if at all. It is this reasoning why abstinence is being taught within the Christian community today and around the world. Biblically speaking, one would think that being against consensual sex among men and women would be the same as being against God. Remember, God said "be fruitful and multiple," not just to Adam and Eve (mankind), but to all the sea life and birds of the air. Do they marry? In other words, do they make covenants that are legal and binding?

Genesis 1:21–22

God created great whales, and every living creature…after their kind, and every winged fowl after his kind: and God saw that it was good, and God blessed them, saying, be fruitful, and multiply…

Genesis 1:27-28

So God created man in his own image, in the image of God he created them; male and female and God blessed them, and God said to them, be fruitful, and multiply, and replenish the earth, and subdue it…

Much of what Paul wrote to the various churches was about consensual sex and at times money (the gift, the abundance, bounty, supply, and giving and receiving). Paul seem to be using consensual sex to control his followers, by saying they should abstain, in order to please God, or God is against it, which is clearly a lie based on the first chapter of Genesis, and every male character in the Old Testament Bible that had multiple wives and concubines. Paul gave no logical reason, such as, a plague or disease upon the earth that affected the people in some way that would require them to abstain from sex. The point here is, who does Paul think he is to tell others how and with whom they should or should not have sex, which is a private act?

The problem with Paul as the standard-bearer for Christians is that no one really knows Paul. For example, in the book of Acts, said to be written by Luke, Paul says he's a Jew. In first Corinthians, written by Paul, he pretends to be a Jew. Is Paul a Jew? One thing is clear: You don't have to pretend to be someone who you already are. Unless, you are not who you say you are.

Acts 21:39

Paul said: I am a Jew of Tarsus, a city in Cilicia…

1 Corinthians 9:19–22

I am free from all men, yet have I made myself servant to all, that I might gain the more. **To the Jews I became as a Jew, that I might gain the Jews**; to them that are under the law, as under the law, that I might gain them that are under the law; To them that are without law, as without law…that I might gain them that are without law. To the weak became I as weak, that I might gain the weak: I am made all things to all men, that I might by all means save some.

Again Christians believe that Paul was an apostle of Jesus Christ. According to the scriptures, it depended on who Paul was writing to that defined who he was. (See Appendix 3: Who Does Paul Say He Was) For example, when he wrote to the Thessalonian and Philippian churches, Paul made no mention of being an apostle. In fact, he simply wrote to them as Paul. When he wrote his first letter to the Corinthian and Roman churches, he was called *to be* an apostle. Theologians adding the words "*to be*" changes how you see Paul. The statement "called *to be* an apostle" can mean one of two things: either Paul is an apostle or he would be in the future. However, when you remove the words "to be," Paul was called an apostle, not that he was or would ever be an apostle. When Paul wrote his second letter to the Corinthian, Colossian, and Ephesian churches, Paul said he was an apostle of Jesus Christ by the will of God. When Paul wrote his first letter to Timothy, his son, he was an apostle of Jesus Christ by the commandment of God our Savior and Lord Jesus Christ. Therefore, depending on whom Paul was writing to and trying to persuade, he tailored who he was for his own gain, because he believed he was all things to all men.

Many church leaders build up Paul as being equal to God, quoting him as though he was God, and making everything he wrote God-driven and purposeful when, in fact, Paul was mentally unstable, based on his own writings. Now remember, it is this same Paul who wrote to the church in Rome blaming "sin" for his own actions, as though he was possessed.

Romans 7:15-20
> For that which I do, I allow not: for what I would, that do I not; but what I hate, that do I. If then I do that which I would not, I consent to the law that it is good. Then it is no more I that do it, but sin that dwelleth in me. For I know that in

me (that is, in my flesh,) dwells no good thing: for the will is present with me; but how to perform that which is good, I find not. For the good that I would, I do not: but the evil which I would not, that I do. Now if I do that I would not, it is no more I that do it, but sin that dwelleth in me.

Now just imagine for a moment, if anyone other than Paul was to say exactly what he wrote in Romans 7:15–20, word for word, concerning anything that he or she had done, such as commit rape, murder, or armed robbery. Would you believe this person? For sure, you would think that person was mentally ill or delusive, in addition to not taking responsibility for his or her own action(s).

Again, it was this same Paul who used God to project his own actions of coveting onto men and women in or desiring a same-sex relationship to disparage them.

Romans 1:26-27.

For this cause God gave them up to vile affections: for even their women did change the natural use into that which is against nature: And likewise also the men, leaving the natural use of the woman, burned in their lust one toward another; men with men working that which is unseemly, and receiving in themselves that recompense of their error which was meet...

Now, the reason Paul gave for writing his letter to the Romans was that he believed that God had given him "grace," to minister the "gospel of God" to the Gentiles in order to present the "Gentiles" as an acceptable offering to God.

Romans 15:15-16

> Nevertheless, brethren, I have written more boldly to you in some sort, as putting you in mind, because of the grace that is given to me of God, that I should be the minister of Jesus Christ to the Gentiles, ministering the gospel of God, that the offering up of the Gentiles might be acceptable, being sanctified by the Holy Ghost…

Romans 15:18-19

> For I will not dare to speak of any of those things which Christ has not worked by me, to make the Gentiles obedient, by word and deed, Through mighty signs and wonders, by the power of the Spirit of God… I have fully preached the gospel of Christ.

The same grace that Paul believed that God had given him in Romans 15:15-16, to minister the gospel of God, is the same grace he believed God gave him in 2 Corinthians 12:9 (**"<u>My grace is sufficient for you</u>: for my strength is made perfect in weakness"**), concerning his thorn in the flesh, which made absolutely no sense. Nevertheless, as a minister of the gospel of God, Paul believed that Jesus Christ was speaking through, by, or in him in order to make the Gentiles obedient. In other words, what Paul is saying was whatever he says should be considered the gospel of God or the absolute truth, because Jesus Christ, the Son of God, was speaking through, by, or in him. As a result, Paul seemed to believe that everything he said was in essence the Word of God.

Again remember, the church at Corinth challenged Paul, because they wanted proof that Jesus Christ was speaking in him (2 Corinthians 13:3). Then in Romans, chapter 1, Paul believed he had the authority to speak for God or as God, against men and women in a same-sex relationship saying,

Romans 1:24

* **God also gave them up to uncleanness...**

Romans 1:26

* **God gave them up to vile affections...**

Romans 1:28

* **God gave them over to a reprobate mind...**

Everything Paul wrote in Romans 1:26-32, concerning same-sex relations in the first chapter of Romans, continued on into the second chapter, where Paul stated that those who obey his truth seek eternal life or the promise of eternal life. Those who do not obey will receive indignation, wrath, tribulation and anguish, because God would judge all men based on <u>his gospel</u>. Not the Gospel of Matthew, Mark, Luke and John: The first four books of the New Testament Bible, which gives Christian an account of Jesus Christ and his teachings.

Romans 2:7–11, 16

> To them who by patient continuance in well doing seek for glory and honor and immortality, eternal life: To them that are contentious, and do not obey the truth, but obey unrighteousness, indignation and wrath, Tribulation and anguish, upon every soul of man that do evil, of the Jew first, and also of the Gentile; but glory, honor, and peace, to every man that work good, to the Jew first, and also to the Gentile: For there is no respect of persons with God... **In the day,**

when God shall judge the secrets of men by Jesus Christ according to <u>my gospel</u>.

"**Gospel:** 1. set of beliefs: a set of beliefs held strongly by a group or person 2. absolute truth: something believed to be absolutely and unquestionably true"
Encarta ® World English Dictionary

Therefore, Paul was telling the Gentiles to follow him, not Jesus Christ, and obey his gospel. Ask yourself: Why would God give Paul grace to preach his gospel to anyone? Especially, when this same Paul never dealt with his own issues with sin, blamed God for his own actions of coveting, never repented or took responsibility for his own evil actions, and abolished God's laws and commandments.

It should be clear that Paul was mentally unstable. Even, the *Wycliffe Bible Encyclopedia* and the *Holman Bible Dictionary*, both put forth suggestions implying that Paul could have suffered from some sort of brain disorder, such as, "epilepsy," "nervous exhaustion," or "hysteria." Nevertheless, Christians are taught by church leaders to rely on Paul's teachings, for spiritual guidance. Why? What exactly is Paul offering the Gentiles (who are Christians), for their obedience? Grace? It is clear, what Christians expect when they follow Jesus Christ, rightly or wrongly, and that is eternal life.

John 10:27-28

My sheep hear my voice, and I know them, and they follow me: I give to them eternal life; and they shall never perish, neither shall any man pluck them out of my hand.

CHAPTER 12

AFTER ALL

THERE HAVE BEEN MORE THAN thirty years of TV evangelism, preaching, and teaching against same-sex relationships and marriage. One might think that Jonathan and David's relationship would have been discussed once or twice when the topic was mentioned. Their love story is not taught at all within the Christian community and it should be, in support of same-sex relationships and marriage.

Perhaps their love story is not taught because of who David was. David played an important role throughout both the Old and New Testaments. The love story of Jonathan and David in the Old Testament would be a great contradiction in the New Testament, especially with Paul's letter to the Romans, because their love story strongly implies a romantic, loving, and emotional relationship between two men, in addition to being a modern-day example for those who are in or desire a same-sex relationship or marriage.

Some individuals may identify with the character Jonathan who was told by his father, King Saul, that he was confused because of his love for David, the son of Jesse.

1 Samuel 20:30

> Then Saul's anger was kindled against Jonathan, and he said
> to him, you son of the perverse rebellious woman, do not I
> know that you have chosen the son of Jesse to your own con-
> fusion, and to the confusion of your mother's nakedness?

King Saul's crude remarks against his son Jonathan should be compared to God's love toward David. Paul pondered this question in
Romans 8:31: "If God be for us, who can be against us?" Biblically,
God and Jesus stood with David and who he was as a person, after
he made a covenant of love with another man. So, who are we to be
against it?

As true believers we acknowledge that God is love; and He continues
to love and protect us, even when we do not believe we are worthy
to be loved. Now are we to pick and choose who we will love and
protect? Many Christians should be reminded that God loved David
and did not see him as confused, weak, or less than any other man,
but as a strong fighter who was worthy to be king.

Many men and women in a same-sex relationship or desiring one,
grow up under the banner of Christianity, denying their true nature
and lying to themselves, whether in marriage or living single. It is
religion that put Christians and non-Christians into a mold, in which
they do not fit. They spend much or all of their lives trying to scratch
and claw their way out, but they don't know how. Some never break
the mold that binds them out of fear of intimidation, isolation, or
not being loved. As a result, they just follow, letting others define
who they are or who they should be. Accepting that there might be
something wrong with them, they lie to themselves all the more.

They begin living under a cloud of shame and guilt, believing that everything they do or feel is wrong. They are spiritually beaten and broken down mentally and emotionally, being told by strangers, friends, family, and spiritual leaders repeatedly that same-sex relations are wrong, perverse, sick, and evil, and that God and Jesus is against it.

Some parents blame each other, themselves, or their children when they learn that their child is attracted to someone of the same sex. They rely on scriptures for guidance that they don't completely understand and deceive themselves and their children with mixed messages rooted in ignorance. One moment, loving them, caring for them, feeding them, and clothing them. The next moment, parents are throwing away their children to the streets, leaving them homeless and alone because they cannot accept them for who they really are, young boys and young girls who are attracted to someone of the same sex.

Now, could it be that some Christians believe that Jesus is requiring them to disregard and/or separate themselves from their family members who do not believe or live as they do? Yes. They may come to this conclusion based on the gospels of Matthew and Luke.

In Matthew's Jesus said he came to divide the household, then illustrated his teachings to his followers, two chapters later, when he disregarded or ignored his own mother, the Virgin Mary and his brothers, stating that his disciples (followers) were his family.

Matthew 10:34–38

Do not suppose that I have come to bring peace to the earth. I did not come to bring peace, but a

sword. **For I am come to set a man at variance against his father, and the daughter against her mother, and the daughter in law against her mother in law. And a man's foes shall be they of his own household. He that loves his father or mother more than me is not worthy of me: and he that loves his son or daughter more than me is not worthy of me. And he that take not his cross, and follow after me, is not worthy of me.**

Again,

Matthews 12:46-50

While he yet talked to the people, behold, his mother and his brothers stood without, desiring to speak with him. Then someone said to Jesus, Behold, your mother and brothers stand without, desiring to speak with you. He answered and said to him that told him: **Who is my mother? Who are my brothers?** Then he stretched forth his hand toward his disciples, and said: **Behold my mother and my brothers! For whosoever shall do the will of my Father which is in heaven, the same is my brother, and sister, and mother.**

In the gospel of Luke, Jesus taught his followers to hate their own flesh and blood, including their own life, and to give up everything for him.

Luke 14:25

And there went great multitudes with him: and he turned, and said to them: **If any man come to me, and hate not**

his father, and mother, and wife, and children, and brother, and sisters, yes, and his own life also, he cannot be my disciple. Whosoever does not bear his cross, and come after me, cannot be my disciple...

Luke 14: 33

So likewise, whosoever...that forsake not all that he has, he cannot be my disciple.

Nonetheless, despite these teachings, many Christians and non-Christians today love their mothers, fathers, sisters, brother, spouse, and children, regardless of what they believe, who they follow, or who they love. Many Christians may believe that Christianity as a whole is about focusing on the family and family values. However, if they believe that the parents should be against their children, who do not believe as they do, then according to the scriptures the family should and will be divided.

After all, much of what is written about sex in the New Testament comes from Paul's letters. Every letter Paul wrote was a personal letter to the church he was trying to influence and not to Christians today. Therefore, it should be clear that Paul was against consensual sex and deemed others who have sex outside of his defined parameters of marriage, unrighteous. Many churches under the banner of Christianity try to project Paul's gospel onto Christians and non-Christians around the world today. Why? There is no greater example in the Bible concerning consensual sex other than David. He was an adulterer who had multiple wives, many concubines (single ladies), and Jonathan, a man whose love to David was greater than his love of all women. Jonathan and David's relationship in the Bible should be an example for all Christians and non-Christians, that same-sex relationships and marriage may be God's will.

The story of Sodom and Gomorrah inspires much of what is written or spoken within the Christian community about same-sex relations. It was Paul's assertion that linked men and women who have consensual same-sex relations to the deviant sexual behavior of Sodom and Gomorrah in Romans 1:27, therefore demonizing men and women in or desiring a consensual same-sex relationship or marriage. Every church leader who continues to perpetuate Paul's hate speech against men and women who have consensual same-sex relations, or the lie that Sodom and Gomorrah is about consensual sex among men and not rape, are liars and should be called out as liars, for not teaching and preaching the truth and taking away the focus from the criminal act of rape against men, women, and children around the world today.

It is imperative for Christians to question what they believe, why they believe it, and who they believe, and not just accept what is being preached from every pulpit, but study what he or she says and believes to be the "Word of God" for themselves.

CHAPTER 13

WHAT IS A HOMOSEXUAL?

———◆———

"Homosexual: of or having sexual desire for
those of the same sex"
Webster's New World Compact

———◆———

"Homosexual: 1. attracted to same sex: sexually attracted to
members of the same sex 2. of homosexuality: relating to sexual
attraction or activity among members of the same sex"
Encarta ® World English Dictionary

What does it mean to be a homosexual? By definition, a homosexual is someone who has a sexual attraction to, sexual desires for,
or sexual activity with another person or persons of the same sex.

Sexual Attraction: is a visual pleasure of wanting and imagining
the other person or persons sexually based on persona, looks, walk,
and so forth.

Sexual Desire: is the imagination expressing a wanted sexual pleasure.

Sexual Activity: is a physical interaction of a sexual nature such as kissing, and oral, vaginal or anal copulation.

Now the question is: How do you define a person as a homosexual based on the definition listed above and the examples below?

#1

* A man marries his wife at the age of thirty, and they have four children together. Throughout their twenty-two years of marriage, he had always been sexually attracted to men and desired them day and night, but never committed a sexual act with another man. Is he a homosexual?

If no, then the definition of a homosexual is null and void because there was sexual attraction and desire. If yes, then a person's thoughts or imaginations would define who he or she was. Then the definition is flawed because having the thought or imagination to kill or rape does not make you a murderer or a rapist. Therefore, sexual attraction to and sexual desire for someone of the same sex as an identifier of a person being a homosexual is a self-applied label.

#2

* An eighteen-year-old young man, who had always dated females throughout his high school years, goes to college and has sex with his male roommate in his first year, only once. Afterward he continued dating females. He later graduated and met a woman, and he never desired to be with another man. Is he a homosexual?

If no, then the definition of a homosexual is null and void because there was sexual activity or relations between two people of the same sex. If yes, the sexual act itself, regardless of when it happened, would define an individual as a homosexual for the rest of his or her life. Therefore, the word "homosexual" is only a label.

#3

⁋   What if a man physically rapes another man? Is the man who was raped a homosexual?

If no, then the definition of a homosexual is null and void because there was sexual activity or relations between two people of the same sex. If yes, then the sexual act itself, regardless of how it happened, would define an individual as a homosexual for the rest of his or her life. Therefore, the word "homosexual" is only a label.

#4

⁋   A man's only fantasy was to have sex with two women at the same time. His loving wife and her best friend agreed to satisfy his every desire, including both women having sex with each other, on this one occasion. Are the woman homosexuals?

If no, then the definition of a homosexual is null and void because there was sexual activity or relations between two people of the same sex. If yes, then the sexual act itself, regardless of why it happened, would define both individuals as a homosexual for the rest of their lives. Therefore, the word "homosexual" is only a label.

#5

* What if a woman has a sexual relationship with another woman whom she is attracted to and desires every day and night all the days of her life? Are they homosexuals?

If no, then the definition of a homosexual is null and void because there was sexual activity or relations between two people of the same sex. If yes, then the sexual act itself, regardless of when, how, or why it happened, but the fact that it happened would define both individuals as homosexuals all the days of their lives. Therefore, taking all into account, the word "homosexual" is nothing more than a label.

Human beings are sexual beings. Remove all labels.

PART 2

CHAPTER 14

THE COMPARISON
(A Tale of Two Rapes)

———————

A FABLE IS A FICTIONAL story that may contain supernatural, mythological, mystical, or legendary characters and events to teach a lesson. The story of Sodom and Gomorrah has all the characteristics
of a fable: the mythological rain of fire and brimstone falling from a
mystical heaven that destroys all human life and land within two cities by an all-powerful God, who sends two men (witnesses) toward
the city of Sodom who enter as angels with superhuman abilities to
blind men at will. Lot, who is legendary, is the main reoccurring
character always in need of being saved. This is what some of the
great fairy tales are made of.

What further supports the fact that Sodom and Gomorrah is nothing
more than a fable is the story, The Concubine. When you compare
Sodom and Gomorrah to The Concubine, they appear to be two separate stories, yet, verse by verse; they are the same within the cen-
tral theme of the story, as highlighted in the following Comparison
Chart. For example, both stories begin with a homeowner inviting in
strangers. The wicked men of the city surround the house where the
strangers were staying. They demand the stranger(s) be brought out
so they could rape them. The homeowners plead for the stranger(s)
not to be harmed. The homeowners, who are fathers, offer up their

daughter(s) to be gang-raped, by all the men of the city, in defense of the male stranger(s). Looking at both stories very carefully, one thing stands out: one is a mirror copy of the other in many aspects, even though one verse may be more dramatic than another verse.

THE COMPARISON CHART	
The Concubine	**Sodom and Gomorrah**
1) The Old man invited two strangers into his home, the Levite and his concubine, to stay with him, wash their feet and eat:	1) Lot invited the two strangers into his home to stay with him, wash their feet and eat:
Judges 19:21 So he brought him into his house, and gave provender unto the asses: and they washed their feet, and did eat and drink.	Genesis 19:2-3 And he said, Behold now, my lords, turn in, I pray you, into your servant's house, and tarry all night, and wash your feet, and ye shall rise up early, and go on your ways. And they said, Nay; but we will abide in the street all night. And he pressed upon them greatly; and they turned in unto him, and entered into his house; and he made them a feast, and did bake unleavened bread, and they did eat.
2) The angry mob of men surrounded the Old man's house and demanded that the man be brought out:	2) The angry mob of men surrounded Lot's house and demanded that the men be brought out:
Judges 19:22 Now as they were making their hearts merry, behold, the men of the city, certain sons of Belial, beset the house round about, and beat at the door, and spake to the master of the house, the old man, saying, Bring forth the man that came into thine house, that we may know him.	Genesis19:4-5 But before they lay down, the men of the city, even the men of Sodom, compassed the house round, both old and young, all the people from every quarter: And they called unto Lot, and said unto him, Where are the men which came in to thee this night? bring them out unto us, that we may know them.

THE COMPARISON CHART	
The Concubine	Sodom and Gomorrah
3) The Old man pleaded for the stranger inside his house, not to be harmed.	3) Lot pleaded for the two strangers inside his house, not to be harmed.
Judges 19:23 And the man, the master of the house, went out unto them, and said unto them, Nay, my brethren, nay, I pray you, do not so wickedly; seeing that this man is come into mine house, do not this folly.	Genesis 19:6-7 And Lot went out at the door unto them, and shut the door after him, And said, I pray you, brethren, do not so wickedly.
4) The Old man offered his daughter and the Concubine to the angry mob in place of the stranger that came into his home.	4) Lot offered his two virgin daughters to the angry mob in place of the two strangers (men/angels) that came into his home.
Judges 19:24 Behold, here is my daughter a maiden, and his concubine; them I will bring out now, and humble ye them, and do with them what seemeth good unto you: but unto this man do not so vile a thing.	Genesis 19:8 Behold now, I have two daughters which have not known man; let me, I pray you, bring them out unto you, and do ye to them as is good in your eyes: only unto these men do nothing; for therefore came they under the shadow of my roof.

Why tell either of these stories about an attempted gang rape of men and the gang rape of a women, unless there is something more to both stories? When you analyze each fable individually, they appear to be about sexual immorality, men wanting to gang-rape other men. However, nothing is as it seems. When you analyze both fables together as to how they may relate to each other, a whole new understanding comes to light. There is one clear lesson that the writer(s) of Sodom and Gomorrah and The Concubine are trying to teach us.

About Women

The lesson you learn from the writer(s) of both fables, Sodom and Gomorrah and The Concubine, is that women had no rights. The women in both stories were truly instruments used by and for men. Fathers put forth their daughter(s) in defense of men who were strangers to be gang-raped. One would assume, the daughter(s) he raised, protected, saw grow up before his own eyes, broke bread with at the dinner table, spoke with everyday, and who lived under their father's roof, were made worthless in one statement.

Lot (Sodom and Gomorrah): "Let me bring them out to you, and you can do what you like with them."

Old Man (The Concubine): "Behold, here is my daughter a maiden, and his concubine; them I will bring out now, and humble them, and do with them what seem good to you"

The writer(s) never explained why Lot and the old man were willing to give up their daughter(s) for strangers. However, the *Holman Bible Dictionary* tries to explain Lot's behavior toward his daughters, as "the lesser of two evils," under the term "homosexuality."

Homosexuality
Holman Bible Dictionary

* "Sexual preference for and sexual behavior between members of the same sex, considered to be an immoral life-style

and behavior pattern throughout the biblical revelation. Only heterosexual preference and behavior patterns are approved in Scripture as conforming to God's plan in the creation of man and woman. Moreover, all sexual behavior is to take place in the context of marriage. Sex is considered good so long as it takes place within these parameters."

❧ "(v. 5) mentions specifically the homosexual intentions of the men of Sodom. Lot considers this behavior wicked (v. 7). Raping his daughters was considered the lesser of two evils (v. 8)."

To be clear, the *Holman Bible Dictionary* appears to be saying that a women being gang-raped is "the lesser of two evils" when compared to a man being gang-raped, because they believe that sex between a man and a woman conforms to God's plan. The word "rape" does not appear in the King James Version of the Bible. However, statements such as "forced her," and "abused her" are used to describe a sexual assault, which is rape. Consensual sex between a man and a woman would mean both or all parties are in agreement with the sex or type of sex they would have. If the man took the woman and forced her, or abused her, it is rape. The same would apply if it was between two men instead of a man and a woman. It's not who is raped that makes it rape. Rape is rape.

There is no greater example in the entire Bible of what rape really is other than the story, The Concubine, where the angry mob came for the Levite to force him or abuse him, by ripping his clothes from his body; beating him with their fists; holding him down; forcing their lips upon his mouth and body; forcing their penises into his mouth to be sucked dry; and forcing their penises inside his rectum over and over again until every man was satisfied. Now, the Levite may have been their preference to dominate sexually; however, they took what was given, the woman, and raped her to death, forever solidifying that rape is about lust, anger, physical control, and violence.

It would appear the writer(s) chose rape as their theme in both fables, Sodom and Gomorrah and The Concubine, to capture your attention and to make it clear that men are dominant compared to the women. Using the daughters demonstrated the man's dominance in the human hierarchy, even to the extent of a father discarding his own daughter(s) for the protection and well-being of a male stranger. The writer(s) made it clear in the story of Sodom and Gomorrah that men should always be protected over women. In the story, The Concubine, the writer(s) clearly demonstrated that men should always be protected over the women, even if it kills them.

Therefore, the lesson that the writer(s) of both stories wanted to convey was not same-sex relations (to be specific), fornication, or bestiality, but male dominance.

The Kingdom of Heaven

Jesus said,

Matthew 13:24–30

The kingdom of heaven is likened to a man which sow good seed in his field: But while men slept, his enemy came and sowed tares among the wheat, and went his way. But when the blade was sprung and brought forth fruit, then appeared the tares also. So the servants of the householder came and said to him, Sir, did you not sow good seed in your field? From where then has it tares? He said to them, an enemy has done this. The servants said to him, Will you rather we go and gather them up? But he said, No; lest while you gather up the tares you root up also the wheat with them. Let both grow together until the harvest: and in the time of harvest I will say to the reapers, gather together first the tares and bind them in bundles to burn them: but gather the wheat into my barn.

APPENDIX

APPENDIX I

New Testament Books (Current Order)

Matthew
Mark
Luke
John
Acts
Romans
1 Corinthians
2 Corinthians
Galatians
Ephesians
Philippians
Colossians
1 Thessalonians
2 Thessalonians
1 Timothy
2 Timothy
Titus
Philemon
Hebrews
James
1 Peter
2 Peter
1 John
2 John
3 John
Jude
Revelation

New Testament Books (Chronological Order)

Matthew
Thessalonians
2 Thessalonians
Mark
1 Corinthians
2 Corinthians
Romans
Galatians
1 Peter
James
Luke
Ephesians
Philippians
Philemon
Hebrews
Colossians
Acts
1 Timothy
Titus
2 Timothy
2 Peter
Jude
John
1 John
2 John
3 John
Revelation

Note: An Internet search for books of the Bible or the chronological order of the books of the Bible will yield several different results. Therefore, the information provided above should be considered as just another search and treated as general information.

APPENDIX II

New Testament Books (By Authors)

Author:	Book(s):	# of books Written
Matthew	The Gospel of Matthew	1
Mark	The Gospel of Mark	1
Luke	The Gospel of Luke	2
	The Book of Acts	
John	The Gospel of John	5
	1 John	
	2 John	
	3 John	
	Revelations	
Paul	Romans	14
	1 Corinthians	
	2 Corinthians	
	Galatians	
	Ephesians	
	Philippians	
	Colossians	
	1 Thessalonians	
	2 Thessalonians	
	1 Timothy	
	2 Timothy	
	Titus	
	Philemon	
	Hebrew	
Peter	1 Peter	2
	2 Peter	
James	James	1
Jude	Jude	1

APPENDIX III

WHO DOES PAUL SAY HE WAS?
To the Churches

Hebrews	No introduction
Philippians	No mention of Paul being an apostle Paul and Timotheus, the servants of Jesus Christ, to all the saints in Christ Jesus which are at Philippi, with the bishops and deacons:
1 Thessalonians	No mention of Paul being an apostle Paul, and Silvanus, and Timotheus, to the church of the Thessalonians *(which is)* in God the Father and *(in)* the Lord Jesus Christ: Grace *be* to you, and peace, from God our Father, and the Lord Jesus Christ.
2 Thessalonians	No mention of Paul being an apostle Paul, and Silvanus, and Timotheus, to the church of the Thessalonians in God our Father and the Lord Jesus Christ.
1 Corinthians	Paul, called *(to be)* an apostle of Jesus Christ through the will of God, and Sosthenes *our* brother,
Romans	Paul a servant of Jesus called *(to be)* an Apostle.

Galatians	Paul, an apostle, (not of men, neither by man, but by Jesus Christ, and God the Father, who raised him from the dead)
2 Corinthians	Paul, an apostle of Jesus Christ by the will of God
Ephesians	Paul, an apostle of Jesus Christ by the will of God
Colossians	Paul, an apostle of Jesus Christ by the will of God

To Actual Persons

Philemon	Paul, a prisoner of Jesus Christ
Titus	Paul, a servant of God, and an apostle of Jesus Christ, according to the faith of God's elect, and the acknowledging of the truth which is after godliness
1 Timothy	Paul, an apostle of Jesus Christ by the commandment of God our Saviour, and Lord Jesus Christ, (*which is*) our hope
2 Timothy	Paul, an apostle of Jesus Christ by the will of God, according to the promise of life which is in Christ Jesus

APPENDIX IV

Sources
(By Reference Book)

Encarta ® World English Dictionary

"Autocracy." *Encarta ® World English Dictionary*, 1998–2005.

"Covet." *Encarta ® World English Dictionary*, 1998–2005.

"Gospel." *Encarta ® World English Dictionary*, 1998–2005.

"Homosexual." *Encarta ® World English Dictionary*, 1998–2005.

"Lust." *Encarta ® World English Dictionary*, 1998–2005.

"Prostitute." *Encarta ® World English Dictionary*, 1998–2005.

"Romantic." *Encarta ® World English Dictionary*, 1998–2005.

"Sodomite." *Encarta ® World English Dictionary*, 1998–2005.

"Sodomy." *Encarta ® World English Dictionary*, 1998–2005.

"Unnatural." *Encarta ® World English Dictionary*, 1998–2005.

Holman Bible Dictionary for Windows

"Christian." *Holman Bible Dictionary for Windows*, version 1.0g, 1994.

"Covenant." *Holman Bible Dictionary for Windows*, version 1.0g, 1994.

"Homosexuality." *Holman Bible Dictionary for Windows*, version 1.0g, 1994.

"Israel." *Holman Bible Dictionary for Windows*, version 1.0g, 1994.

"Sodom and Gomorrah." *Holman Bible Dictionary for Windows*, version 1.0g, 1994.

"Sodomite." *Holman Bible Dictionary for Windows*, version 1.0g, 1994.

"Thorn in the Flesh." *Holman Bible Dictionary for Windows*, version 1.0g, 1994.

"Wrath." *Holman Bible Dictionary for Windows*, version 1.0g, 1994.

Webster's Encyclopedic Unabridged Dictionary

"Covet." *Webster's Encyclopedic Unabridged Dictionary*, 2nd ed., 1993.

"Lust." *Webster's Encyclopedic Unabridged Dictionary*, 2nd ed., 1993.

"Rape." *Webster's Encyclopedic Unabridged Dictionary*, 2nd ed., 1993.

"Sodomite." *Webster's Encyclopedic Unabridged Dictionary*, 2nd ed., 1993.

"Sodomy." *Webster's Encyclopedic Unabridged Dictionary*, 2nd ed., 1993.

"Unnatural." *Webster's Encyclopedic Unabridged Dictionary*, 2nd ed., 1993.

"Wrath." *Webster's Encyclopedic Unabridged Dictionary*, 2nd ed., 1993.

Webster's New World Compact School and Office Dictionary

"Homosexual." *Webster's New World Compact School and Office Dictionary*, 1995.

"Rape." *Webster's New World Compact School and Office Dictionary*, 1995.

Wikipedia, The Free Encyclopedia,

"Sodomite." *Wikipedia, The Free Encyclopedia*, Modified 6/16. Web. Accessed 1/17

"Sodomy." *Wikipedia, The Free Encyclopedia*. Web. Accessed 1/17.

Wycliffe Bible Encyclopedia

"David." *Wycliffe Bible Encyclopedia*, 1975.

"Gomorrah." *Wycliffe Bible Encyclopedia*, 1975.

"Israel." *Wycliffe Bible Encyclopedia*, 1975.

"Jonathan." *Wycliffe Bible Encyclopedia*, 1975.

"Sodom." *Wycliffe Bible Encyclopedia*, 1975.

"Sodomite." *Wycliffe Bible Encyclopedia*, 1975.

"Thorn in the Flesh." *Wycliffe Bible Encyclopedia*, 1975.

"Wrath." *Wycliffe Bible Encyclopedia*, 1975.

www.ingramcontent.com/pod-product-compliance
Lightning Source LLC
LaVergne TN
LVHW051046080426
835508LV00019B/1725